"Bill Riley's carefully observed and often lyrical book makes us feel what's at stake for the players, coaches, and families of twenty-first-century Milan. We're given access to the sounds and sights of the small-town gym: those strangely beautiful and often struggling cathedrals of Indiana's state religion. And we watch as the town and the team work to forge a new identity while shadowboxing with the mythology of the miracle of Milan. This book is an important addition to the literature of basketball."

—Susan Neville, author of *Butler's Big Dance: The Team, the Tournament, and Basketball Fever*

"In this mesmerizing book about hope, dreams, and community, Bill Riley creates an unforgettable portrait of tiny Milan, Indiana, a town sliding into poverty and lost illusions but still carried by the memory of one long-ago championship season. Writing with steely honesty, rich empathy, and deep intelligence, Riley explores the heartland of contemporary America and tests the endurance of a particularly American dream."

—Erin McGraw, author of *Better Food for a Better World: A Novel*

"For a game that is so centered around arcs and geometry, numbers and statistics, there is a permeating mythos that transcends the game of basketball—of shots that go in from impossible angles, dead spots on the floor, ghosts in the rafters. Riley's book is an examination of what happens when the odds are defied: instead of the game being forever changed, the anomaly resets—that sometimes instead of focusing on the outlier, there is beauty and fascination found in the status quo, the consistency of layup lines, the players and coaches scrapping to break even."

—Brian Oliu, author of *Enter Your Initials for Record Keeping*

"Here's a book that reveals something about what makes a young man keep playing for a team that he suspects will most likely lose its next game, while introducing us to a coach who tries to right the ship while knowing the same thing. This is a story about losing, but it's not about losers. It's about grit, and getting back up."   —Greg Schwipps, author of *What This River Keeps*

"This book takes us to the small town that inspired *Hoosiers,* that Hollywood crowd-pleaser, to measure the burden of a once and former glory. In mellifluous prose, Riley shows us that it takes as much humility as grit and determination to live under the shadow of a nearly sixty-year-old sports legend. Riley shows us that the real drama of sports less often lies in the last-minute shot than in the long run of acceptance of circumstances that are usually beyond our control."

—Kirk Curnutt, author of *Raising Aphrodite*

THE MILAN MIRACLE

THE MILAN MIRACLE

THE TOWN THAT *HOOSIERS* LEFT BEHIND

BILL RILEY

AN IMPRINT OF
INDIANA UNIVERSITY PRESS
Bloomington & Indianapolis

This book is a publication of

Quarry Books
an imprint of
Indiana University Press
Office of Scholarly Publishing
Herman B Wells Library 350
1320 East 10th Street
Bloomington, Indiana 47405 USA

iupress.indiana.edu

Manufactured in the United States of
America

Cataloging information is available from the
Library of Congress

ISBN 978-0-253-02089-5 (paperback)
ISBN 978-0-253-02095-6 (ebook)

1   2   3   4   5   21   20   19   18   17   16

FOR SARAH AND ARTHUR,
my favorites to root for

The Philistine came on and drew near to David, with his shield-bearer in front of him. When the Philistine looked and saw David, he disdained him, for he was only a youth, ruddy and handsome in appearance. The Philistine said to David, "Am I a dog, that you come to me with sticks?" 1 Samuel 17: 41–43 (NRSV)

CONTENTS

ACKNOWLEDGMENTS

To the people of Milan, especially the Voss family, the Layden family, Jeff Stutler, Tyler Theising, Randy Combs, Richard Healy, John Prifogle, Linda White Baurley, the team, the parents, the school, the town: thank you. You let me into your life for a year, and I hope I've done right by you. Your story—not just the 1954 version—is worth telling and considering.

Josh, Jill, and Noah Blankinship, thank you for treating me like a friend when all I was looking for was a good story. Your humanity—in your care for Milan's students and each other—is real Hoosier hospitality. Thanks for being so passionate about what you do.

To the team, especially Ethan Voss, Braden Voss, Alex Layden, and Logan Alloway, thanks for letting me in on the ride, thanks for letting me root for you, thanks for the hope a teenager brings, thanks for letting me see you cry on a dark bus somewhere on State Road 101. Thanks for not looking when I did the same.

I had some really good teachers who made me want to live up to their work. For the kind words, the tough words, the harsh words, and the true words, thank you to Erin McGraw, Greg Schwipps, Samuel Autman, Lee Martin, Lee K. Abbott, Michelle Herman, and Andrew Hudgins.

Liz Wyckoff fixed this book and helped me find the humans who were playing all that basketball. She's really the best editor.

Derek Palacio, Gabriel Urza, Clayton Clark, Alex Streiff, Daniel Carter: the Bulleit and Books Boys. Thanks for sharing your work. Thanks for reading mine. We did it. Ferrell and Claire and the Hammer too.

Thank you to Indiana University Press for publishing this book, and to Linda Oblack and Sarah Jacobi for getting this ink on this paper.

Thank you to my parents, who showed me Steve Alford, Robinson vs. Henderson, Damon Bailey, Kojak Fuller, Oskee-Wah-Wah, the Largest High School

Gymnasium in the World, how to root for an underdog, and how to win and lose the Trester Award.

To my wife, Sarah, thanks for putting up with spotty phone service and a big idea, gallons of gas and hours of work away, and for sticking up for my ideas even when I didn't. To Arthur, thanks for the good luck kiss on the book proposal at three weeks old. You're just what I needed.

AUTHOR'S NOTE

In researching this book, I spent hours with the players, parents, coaches, and townspeople of Milan. I came to know them well, through both immersion and my own reflection on their lives. I took pages of handwritten notes, including quotes, descriptions, characters' reactions, and other sensory details. Sometimes I used a tape recorder for pre- and postgame speeches.

When gaps existed in my notes, I relied on my memory and reflections to drive the narrative. At these points, I have tried my best to stay true to the character and the moment. For that reason, I do not consider these moments a fictionalization. However, it should be noted that my reportage and memory are uniquely mine, and some bias may exist based on my knowledge and previous research.

At times, I seek to dramatize this story by letting the reader understand a character's thought process or emotions. I developed these moments through my primary research, my understanding of the character, and informal interviews with the characters. None of these are wholly reliable, but I have done my best to push toward an overall truth in these regards.

THE MILAN MIRACLE

PROLOGUE

The photograph on the poster in Josh Blankinship's office was immediately familiar to me. Behind his cluttered desk and antiquated Dell computer, he had the poster mounted in a cheap black plastic frame, drilled into the cinder-block walls of his office under the home bleachers of Milan High School. The photograph was familiar to me because I, like Josh, was born to Indiana, born to a state that had been basketball-mad for some time. He was one year my senior at twenty-eight years old in 2010, and had also been born to Indiana during a tumultuous time for the state—economic decline, agricultural decline, manufacturing decline. The decline wasn't relegated to the pocketbooks of Indiana's government and residents. Like everything that happened in the state, it affected basketball. Basketball was and continues to be the state's primary diversion. It's the topic of discussion during coffee hours in the basements of churches; it's on the lips of barbershop and library and grocery store patrons. The local school's colors are shoe-polished onto the windows. Even those Hoosiers who hate basketball know it's important to those around them.

Once you smell the dust from the dead corn husks in the air, you know basketball season is near.

The photograph is a black-and-white print of a basketball half-court. A ball is resting near the free throw line. The gym is old: exposed pipes are bolted to the wood-slat walls, and caged fluorescent lights hang from the ceiling, putting buzzer beaters at risk. This gym is not built for buzzer beaters—it's built for motion offenses and possessions spanning half a quarter. It's built for a score of 32–30, the score that the green and red bulbs of the school's old scoreboard usually shows, even when the gym is not being photographed: 32–30, the score of Milan–Muncie Central in 1954 that set this whole story in motion.

The photograph is a picture of Milan, and it isn't. The gym in the photograph is the Hoosier Gym in Knightstown, fifty-eight miles northwest of Milan, Indiana, where Milan's basketball team never even played. It's big-screen fiction. Still, when people see the team photo in the top left of the photograph, they think of Milan.

The boys and the coach in that team photo never existed. And yet their story is the one always told, always understood. The story of Coach Norman Dale and Jimmy Chitwood and Shooter Flatch and Ollie—the characters from the 1986 movie *Hoosiers*—is the Milan story that people know, that people expect to see when they drive an hour west from the Cincinnati airport during a long layover on a Delta Airlines flight. When they walk into the real Milan High School gym, they are underwhelmed. The 1954 state finals trophy rests in a small case built into the wall. The state finals banner, torn and water-damaged, hangs next to a runner-up banner from 1953. The magic—the Hollywood drama—exists only in the fictionalization of the real story.

Until I spent the 2010–11 basketball season with the present-day Milan Indians, I believed that the premise of the movie *Hoosiers* was still reality. I believed that, somewhere in the rolling hills of southern Indiana, small high school teams built of farmboys with clinical jump shots could still beat the city high schools with their fancy warm-ups and big-name coaches and players who attended basketball camps in the summers. I believed the parable that is *Hoosiers,* that if David works hard enough, he kills the Philistine. I watched the movie so many times that I thought David always slung the rock with such precision.

I was raised to believe the story. My earliest memory is sitting in front of my parents' wood-paneled push-button television, watching from my miniature Indiana-red wicker rocking chair as Keith Smart rose above Derrick Coleman and Howard Triche and sank a fifteen-foot jump shot from the baseline. That shot—simply called "The Shot" in Indiana—won the 1986–87 national championship for the Indiana University Hoosiers. I had just turned four years old.

The week that followed was my indoctrination into my state's religion: Hoosier Hysteria. My mother, a second-grade teacher at Riley Elementary School in New Castle, Indiana, brought me to school the following week as they welcomed Indiana's star shooting guard, Steve Alford, home from the national championship in New Orleans. An eight-by-ten print of me and Steve from that day still hangs on my wall with the inscription "To Bill: God Bless. Steve Alford." The smile on my face shows that I know that the man—for that's what the college-aged boy seemed to me then—with his hands on my shoulders, showing off his national championship ring, is the same man who played all forty minutes of the game I watched the previous week, the same man who led the Hoosiers in scoring with twenty-three points that night, the same man whose name and face were printed across the chest of my T-shirt in the photo.

My consequent interest in all things basketball led my parents to reveal more of my state's religion to me. Each year, we would attend the Indiana High School Athletic Association's boys' state finals in the Hoosier Dome in Indianapolis. It didn't matter that my mother's New Castle Trojans or my father's Rochester Zebras or my future high school's team—the Greenfield-Central Cougars—weren't playing in the finals. We rooted for the tradition, picked a side—usually the smallest school in the game—and celebrated. We saw Damon Bailey lead Bedford North Lawrence to a state title, and we saw the beginning of a great rivalry that would extend into college: Alan Henderson's Brebeuf Prep losing to Glenn Robinson's Gary Roosevelt. Later, as players at Indiana and Purdue, respectively, Henderson and Robinson would continue their rivalry. Every time I tuned in to an Indiana-Purdue game during those years, I would think of them as high schoolers. The Indiana-Purdue rivalry is important in Indiana, but high school basketball is still the thing that unites communities across the state. After the state finals games, my parents and I would get into our cars and hurry to turn on the radio broadcast, not listening for who received the Most Valuable Player Award but for who won the Arthur L. Trester Mental Attitude Award. This is why we watched the games featuring boys we didn't know from towns we rarely drove through: to see good, clean hard work rewarded. To this day, when one of my parents says the other "just lost the prestigious Trester Award," it means they lost their cool: on a waitress, on a grocery clerk, on each other.

I came to know about Milan in this way: because, as a Hoosier, I was supposed to know about Milan in the same way I was supposed to know how and where my grandparents were raised, supposed to know the cultural and familial history that made me. On the poster in Josh Blankinship's office, the words "Return to Heaven" are printed in large white font, without a drop of irony. Heaven is this fictional basketball court, representing a period in the state's history, economic and athletic, when times were good—simple, even. Heaven is the best story told about the state, the bootstrap story told in *Hoosiers*.

This book is about a very different story. At times, I'm still not sure which story is real: the story retold about Milan's state championship in 1954 or the sister story delivered in the movie *Hoosiers*. In 2010, as Butler University—the small school from India-no-place that played their home games in the same fieldhouse Ollie measures at the end of *Hoosiers*—advanced to the NCAA championship game, comparisons to Milan's state championship in 1954 were commonplace in the media. Television stations—national and local—sent camera crews to Milan for segments. Bobby Plump, Milan's star player in 1954 and an insurance salesman in Indianapolis, gave interviews. The small schools were at it again, just like the old Milan story.

The rhetoric of this story made me curious. The media seemed to parrot the dramatized story line from *Hoosiers*: that if you worked hard, it didn't matter how big you were—you could win. It made me wonder what was happening in Milan right then.

A quick look at John Harrell's Indiana High School basketball website (a simple but exhaustive online database of Indiana basketball schedules, results, and statistics) told me a different story: Milan was managing only two or three wins a season. Everyone was using Milan as an example for success through hard work, success despite the odds. Where was Milan's present-day fairy tale? What heaven could they possibly return to? I knew I had to find out.

From the first day I contacted the Milan head coach, Josh Blankinship, I was given almost unrestricted access to his team. Josh let me attend coaches' meetings, team practices, games, pre- and postgame talks in the locker room. I was with the team as much as I could be and started to feel like a member of their community. As the team's, the town's, and Josh's comfort with me grew, I came to know the people who have become the characters in this book very well. To the outsider, it might be easy to dismiss the Hoosier Hysteria within this book as undue fervor over "just basketball." But to the insider, I say this: what I reveal in this book that may seem unflattering to the outsider is simply a testament to how amazing the town of Milan is to me. In a struggling rural community, basketball—even the last burst of light from that dying star of small-town community basketball in rural Indiana—still united the town in something.

Even if that something was factions of parents warring against each other and a coach and the school system, it united. Milan had a population of 1,899 according to the 2010 census, and on most nights the 2,076-seat gym was near capacity for home games. People care about basketball in Milan because they dream dreams of success in every measure of the word. Their passion, though possibly misguided, is simply for their past to meet their present.

The gym on Josh Blankinship's poster represents heaven for so many in Indiana and beyond. It is a romanticization of the past and a hope for a return to those good times in the future. In a drafty gym—in thousands of them across the state—ten boys at a time try to dribble and pass and rebound their way back. As Coach Norman Dale famously said after letting out a nervous sigh, *Welcome to Indiana basketball.*

2010–11 Milan Indians

	Varsity		
No.	*Name*	*Grade*	*Height*
3	Logan Alloway	9	5'8"
10	Alex Layden	12	5'10"
11	Braden Voss	11	6'1"
12	Ethan Voss	12	6'3"
13	Zack Lewis	11	6'0"
20	John Herzog	11	6'0"
22	Nick Ryan	11	6'4"
23	Kurtis Kimla	11	6'0"
24	Jake White	11	6'1"
34	Nick Walter	11	6'3"
44	Derek Hornberger	12	6'1"

	Junior Varsity		
No.	*Name*	*Grade*	*Height*
3	Logan Alloway	9	5'8"
4	Joey Davis	10	5'9"
5	Gavin Detraz	9	5'9"
21	Jon Spurlock	9	5'9"
30	Ben Lawhorn	11	6'0"
32	Jon Bixler	9	5'10"
33	Logan Karstetter	9	6'1"
42	Russell Pitts	10	6'3"
50	Patrick Baker	10	6'3"

Varsity coach: Josh Blankinship
JV coach: Jeff Stutler
Freshman coach: Tyler Theising
Managers: Vicky Cunningham, Mary-Kate Jackson, Jamie Altieri, Lydon Horton
Athletic director: John Prifogle

2010–11 Milan Indians Schedule

December 4	at Lawrenceburg
December 7	North Decatur
December 10	at South Decatur
December 17	at Trinity Lutheran
December 18	Waldron
December 21	Hauser
December 30	Southwestern (Hanover College gym)
December 30	South Dearborn (Hanover College gym)
January 5	at South Ripley
January 8	Jac-Cen-Del
January 14	at Rising Sun
January 15	at Oldenburg Academy
January 24	South Ripley
January 28	at Southwestern (Hanover College gym)
January 29	Switzerland County
February 4	Rising Sun
February 10	at Jac-Cen-Del
February 18	Scottsburg
February 22	at Shawe Memorial
February 25	Union County
March 2	Hauser (South Ripley gym)

1

MEASUREMENTS AND PRIORITIES

Preseason: 0–0; Previous Season: 3–17

Barely ten minutes after the electronic bell's beep released students into the hallways and out to their cars and buses on the first chilly day of fall, Logan Alloway was in the Milan Senior High School gym with a basketball. Minutes later, two of his teammates and one of his friends joined him, hiking up the legs of their jeans to get into a defensive stance, driving past volleyball players—whose turn it was to use the court—and kicking the ball out for three-pointers. It might have been the volleyball team's turn to use the gym, but this was first and foremost a basketball court.

Logan was almost five feet nine and just fifteen years old. He wore baggy jeans, an oversized plain black shirt, and loose, untied high-top basketball shoes. Behind him, a ratty 1954 state champions banner hung next to a tattered 1953 state runners-up banner. From my view on the sidelines, the glint of his diamond stud earring was interrupted only by his cocked wrist as he set up another long jump shot.

"He needs to grow four inches," Josh Blankinship told me with a hand over his mouth, interrupting the instrumental of bounce bounce, swish, bounce

bounce bounce, swish. Josh acted as if he were telling me a secret, but it was the worst-kept secret in town. "Four inches and he'd be unstoppable."

But in that moment Logan Alloway was just a freshman basketball player in a gym with a capacity for 2,076 screaming fans in a town of only 1,816, a boy who couldn't play enough basketball or get enough of that gym.

A two-on-two game broke out—Logan and his friend against the two other guys on the team. Logan faked to the basket and crossed the ball through his legs, then stepped back to arc a shot. Next possession, he faked a pass into the post and took a snap shot, quick release. The other team switched their marks, and a taller kid came out to guard Logan, to get a hand in his face. Logan passed the ball down to the post, then flared out to the wing, his left hand around his useless belt, holding his jeans up. As he received a pass, he had already started his shooting motion. Three possessions, nine points.

The boys gave up their end of the court ten minutes into the volleyball team's scheduled practice time, but they left no question about whose gym it was. Logan Alloway was one of four hundred students at Milan High School in 2010, and basketball was one of nineteen varsity sports, but that gym had always been a basketball court above all else.

As I drove into Milan from the east, from the nearest metropolitan area—Cincinnati, just under an hour away—I passed everything most people know about southeastern Indiana. I drove next to the Ohio River, with its barges and muddy water, past the Hollywood Casino in Lawrenceburg, and along the Eads Parkway, which seems to be built for the express purpose of shuttling senior citizens to and from the slot machines on the banks of the river. When I hit Lawrenceburg, I rolled down the windows and smelled the gin and whiskey in the air from Lawrenceburg Distillers Indiana. When Seagram's built the distillery in the mid-1800s, it was the largest in the world. Three years ago, Pernod Ricard sold the plant to Angostura, a move that still threatens to shake this region's already unstable economy. The sweet smell quickly becomes sickeningly so.

I kept driving another thirty minutes up State Road 350 to Milan. That's "MY-len," not anything like its Italian namesake. The town sits to the east of the Ripley County seat, Versailles. That's "Ver-SAILS," not anything like its French namesake.

The fields looked just like the fields that Barbara Hershey and Gene Hackman walked through on the way to their first kiss in *Hoosiers*, the 1986 movie based on Milan's 1954 state basketball championship. *Hoosiers* is set in the fictional town of Hickory, but even as I drove through modern-day Milan, I could tell the producers captured 1950s Milan well.

I knew the town had fallen from its perch as the heart of Hoosier Hysteria in the past few decades, but I believed that people in Milan must still care. Milan, even though I had never visited it before, made me proud to be a Hoosier. I bought into the idea that hard work produced good results. I was never good enough to make my high school basketball team, but I served as my high school radio station's play-by-play announcer. To me, basketball felt like the culture of Indiana, the social event, the center. And I knew this was in no small measure because of the movie *Hoosiers* and that Milan team back in 1954. Basketball made Indiana relevant, and Indiana made basketball relevant.

Milan Junior-Senior High School sits on the edge of town. Only a hundred or so homes fit inside the town limits. Downtown is a thousand-foot-by-thousand-foot square holding a medical clinic, a diner, the town hall, five churches, a funeral home, and a museum commemorating the 1954 state championship. The wood siding on the buildings weeps and hangs. The old asphalt of the roads is prone to potholes in the freeze-thaw-refreeze rhythm of southern Indiana's winters. A meat market sits on the far northwest side of town, and past that, only cows.

The junior high and senior high are connected and share everything but a gym—they each have their own. Behind the school sits the football field, the same field where the members of the Milan Indians football team were starting to crash into each other as I arrived in town, tackling and passing and reading defenses, preparing for their upcoming sectional game against North Decatur High School. The football team was playing well and had beaten much larger local rival Batesville High School already that year. At any other high school in the country, the scene of defensive linemen pushing a blocking sled against the backdrop of red and gold leaves would look like a picture-perfect image of autumn.

I wasn't there for the football, though. I came to Milan because I was curious. A fellow Hoosier, I had grown up hearing about the Milan Miracle. On the night before soccer games in high school, my team would get together and eat spaghetti and watch an inspirational movie. We saved *Hoosiers* for our first tournament game each year. It didn't matter if we were the richest school (we weren't) or the school with the most talent (we weren't). We worked hard; we played as a team. *Hoosiers* told us we could win.

But apparently Milan wasn't watching *Hoosiers*. Despite being the small town's claim to fame, despite being the most-watched David versus Goliath sports movie of all time, Milan's basketball team was no longer David. Well, in some ways they were David, all right: woefully overmatched in both size and talent in almost every game. Maybe Goliath had changed: the small area schools had become midsized consolidated county schools, and the big city schools had become farm teams for semiprofessional AAU college scholarship factories. In any event, Milan hadn't won much lately. Most seasons they struggled to win two games. And yet, we—myself, but also the hordes of reporters from far and wide that remind us each March, when a small school makes a run, that it's been done before and could be done again—hardly noticed. We didn't notice when the hoops on the barns outside of town rusted and weren't repaired. We didn't notice when people and jobs—what few there were to begin with—left Milan. We didn't notice that David didn't seem to be winning much anymore.

I was curious, but mostly I needed to know that the story I had been told, the story I had told, the story I had memorized, still existed. I needed to know—as a small-town Hoosier myself, who put stock in my ability to compete with everyone else—that the underdog could still win.

At Milan High School, autumn meant the men of H&W Sport Shop of Campbellsville, Kentucky, fitting the boys of the Milan Indians basketball team— from middle school to varsity—for their season's shoes. Josh Blankinship sat in a lunchroom chair near the H&W cash box, hand over his forehead as if he had a headache. He scanned the order sheet for the shoe sizes and didn't like what he saw. True, these boys were still growing—their acne and ill-fitting clothes underlined that point. But often a bigger-than-proportional shoe size could predict some future height.

"The average shoe size we sell to basketball teams around this area is a 12," Ronnie said to me as he laced up a pair of shoes on a shrimpy sixth-grader. All Josh was seeing was a bunch of size 9s. At the end of the day, the biggest shoe H&W sold to Milan was a 13 1/2. The smallest went to a seventh-grader who ordered a woman's size 6. The Milan Indians would be starting five guards that year on varsity, and their tallest starter was six four.

The first coaches' meeting of the year, on October 21, started as soon as the football coaches cleared out of the office post-practice. Josh's office didn't smell much different than the varsity football locker room next door. He shared the small office with the football coach, Ryan Langferman, who, at thirty-two, was just four years older than Josh. They seemed to like their office more in the style of a dorm room than a study. Three black helmets with gold-and-white Ms and two sets of shoulder pads lay on the floor in the middle of the office, right in front of a brown leather couch. Notre Dame football posters and calendars hung on the walls instead of Josh's preferred Indiana University basketball. The lockers in the small changing room off the office were filled with Under Armour apparel, and a canister of muscle-building supplement sat on top of the lockers.

Joining Josh was Tyler Theising, the young freshman coach just two years out of school at nearby East Central High; Randy Combs, the former basketball head coach and football defensive coordinator, and now the eighth-grade boys' basketball coach; and Jeff Stutler, an assistant on the football team and the varsity basketball assistant coach. As the football coaches left, the mood in the room turned from jovial to serious. The football team was playing well and currently had six wins and four losses. The previous year, the basketball team had gone three and seventeen.

"Let's be honest with ourselves here, guys," Josh said, leaning back in his chair as he talked with Jeff and Tyler. "Lewis at point, Herzog at the two, Braden at the three, Kurtis at the four, Nick at the five."

Tyler ran his hands over his red hair from back to front, making sure it was lying flat. Jeff stroked his salt-and-pepper goatee.

"That's five juniors, guys. That's five guards. Our top five." Josh was worried. The biggest guy from that group, Nick, was six feet four inches.

"And then I've got Alex Layden and Ethan Voss, our seniors." Five eleven. Six three. "They won't start, and I expect Logan Alloway to start stealing some minutes from them toward the end of the season." Logan Alloway. Five eight. "I bought Layden and Voss's shoes today, those are our seniors. I don't see any way Derek makes the team. His dad's going to be the first one to call when I cut his ass, but he got boxed out by Jared Biddle—yes, five-foot-ten Jared Biddle—last week. We can't keep him."

Josh passed out the meeting agenda and some "team philosophy" papers to the coaches. Each sheet had the Milan Basketball letterhead at the top—in Vegas gold and black—and "Return to Glory" in all caps under the letterhead.

Later, as Josh walked around the Milan gym, it was clear that he understood what Milan meant to the state, and to high school basketball nationwide. Pre-1997, the state basketball championship was an open competition. There were no classes based on schools' sizes, and many small schools faced local giants in their sectionals. It didn't matter if the school's enrollment was two hundred or two thousand: everyone played for the same trophy.

And so tiny Milan High School winning the state championship in 1954 was the stuff of Hollywood. But what *Hoosiers* doesn't reenact, and what actually might be more impressive, is that the team finished second in the state in 1953. Two top teams from one small town.

As much as Hollywood has ignored that state runner-up team, it seems Milan ignores it now. Josh was entering his second year at Milan when he found the state runner-up trophy in the storage attic at the school. He was digging around, creating an inventory of supplies, when there, next to warped basketballs and mildewed practice jerseys, sat a memento of perhaps the second-greatest feat in Indiana sports history.

"I knew we had to display it, but we had to create a space," Josh said, shaking his head. "I mean, look over there." He pointed to a cinder-block wall with about fifty laminated five-by-seven pictures resting on small wooden shelves. "That's our goddamn wall of fame, for crying out loud."

He walked back into the gym and pointed to the state championship banner and the state runner-up banner. They were the same size, about ten feet high and three feet wide, black with gold lettering. The borders were tearing, and water stains distorted the black backgrounds. The edges were frayed. "These things have been moved so many times, stored in attics and closets. They don't get cleaned." Josh was trying to get money raised to restore the banners, but they were the least of the town's, and Josh's, worries.

The biggest problem, the coaches agreed, was the fact that this team was miles behind the other area schools in fundamentals. Passing, dribbling, shooting. One kid came to open gym the week before and employed a push shot. The other area schools didn't have the size problems Milan had—each had at least one kid over six five. A push shot wouldn't do. It would end up in the stands. Cut.

The reputation Milan had around the state and around the country, thanks to *Hoosiers*, conflicted with the reality. The stereotypical player from a school like Milan might have been undersized, with a less-athletic frame, but he was a gym rat, a kid who couldn't stay off the basketball court, shooting in his driveway until the floodlights turned on, then switching to layups.

But thanks to the economic depression, state funding cutbacks, and many other less-visible factors, it was rare to see a kid from Milan with a basketball in his hands.

"The problem is," Josh said, hanging his head, "if I'm not in here at six in the morning and until eight at night with that gym open, they're not playing."

Then Coach admitted an even more shocking truth in this small town famous for the fictional Jimmy Chitwood: "It's the only basketball hoop in Milan."

Of course, it's not the only hoop in Milan, as I found when I drove around town later that day. But it was close: I struggled to find even one goal in a driveway inside the Milan town limits.

There was a time when the economy and schools in Milan were good, and so was the basketball. Coach Jeff Stutler had moved back to Milan, his hometown, with his wife in 1974 and remembered a time when people asked for Milan by name when they were looking to relocate their young families. He sold real estate back then and would field a call a week asking for availability in the Milan school district. There'd rarely be an opening.

Then, of course, there was 1954. That year, the Pierceville Alleycats—four Milan High School students from neighboring Pierceville (population forty-five)—led the Indians to their championship with skills they learned on a makeshift alley court. They, along with their teammates who lived in Milan's big Victorian homes with the hoops in front, played daily. In 1954, Miss Indiana was Milan's own Cecilia Dennis. Milan wasn't just a small town in a small corner of the state. It was the center.

But not now. Logan got his ten minutes in before volleyball practice, and he played when Josh opened up the school courts for the team. There was no shooting hoops before dinner in 2010; there were video games and Facebook (when they could get the internet coverage) and cell phones (in the few spots in town where the towers reached). The biggest thing holding Milan back wasn't that their big hope for the future, Logan Alloway, stood six to twelve inches farther away from the basketball hoop than his equally talented opponents. It was that he was able to stand under that hoop far less often.

2

GROWING UP MILAN

Preseason: 0–0

"They all bounce, they're all round, all the same," Josh shouted from the corner of the Milan High School gym, rolling intermediate-sized basketballs onto the floor. The boys, aged eight to twelve, looked at their mothers and fathers and grandparents who brought them to the first night of the Milan Youth Basketball League, asking with Christmas morning smiles: *Really, I can go shoot on the high school floor?* Before the balls could bounce, then roll, to the other side of the gym, the boys collected them. One boy with Velcro-strapped shoes—the kind a grandfather wears—picked up a rolling ball on a sprint, took half as many dribbles as steps toward a basket, and flailed a shot at the rim. The jump toward the rim was more of a ballet leap than an explosive layup, and the ball hit the underside of the rim, crashing back down on his head. He looked back at the stands at his grandmother, rubbing his head and smiling, then moved to the foul line to shoot an underhanded free throw.

My first tour of Milan—my introduction to not just the political and economic realities the team faced, but also the team itself—hadn't troubled me, but this did. I considered myself something of a hoops junkie; in fact, I think basketball might have saved my life. After I graduated from college—where my participation on its Division III football team as a punter forced me to have some sort of restraint in the face of fried foods and beer—my weight had skyrocketed. By the time I took a job as a fund-raiser at my alma mater two years post-graduation, I weighed 280. I was a hundred pounds heavier than I was supposed to be.

I started playing basketball over lunch with a group of staff members and professors. Our games weren't fast-paced, but everyone ran. We may not have been that good, but we played fundamental basketball. We set screens. We played defense.

I lost sixty-five pounds in a year.

A few years later, as a lecturer at a larger university, I found a similar game. I lost more weight, dipping below two hundred pounds for the first time in my adult life, maybe since middle school. I felt good.

When I started, I could barely make it through one game. Later, at age thirty, I was pushing meetings back later in the afternoon so I could play just one more. Once, I had been a kid who loved basketball but wasn't good enough to play in high school in Indiana, where every team seemed to have a legend. Then, years later, I had refined my jump shot. When I watched on TV, I watched as a player. Finally, that basketball gene that they check for in every Indiana hospital had surfaced.

And when it surfaced, I couldn't get enough. I followed small-town editors on Twitter to get schoolboy scores. I watched and rewatched *Hoosiers* nearly monthly. My wife started to get sick of hearing about how Cody Zeller might save Indiana University. I lived in Pennsylvania, where they have two seasons: football season and winter. Every time I played or watched basketball, I felt like I was home.

And so when I saw the chaos that had descended upon the hallowed court of the Milan Indians, the setting of the original David beats Goliath story, the story I had watched countless times, I cringed.

As mothers came into the gym with their sons to hand off their Youth Basketball League registration and a forty-dollar check (in some cases, no check was attached to the registration, and only an understanding glance was exchanged by Josh and the mother), they apologized for their sons' height. "Well, we're trying to feed him right, and he eats like a horse, but he just ain't growing," one mother said. She shook her head and smoothed her son's hair. Poor baby, the gesture said, another small Milan basketball player.

Josh knew some of the boys by name. This was the second year of the Milan Youth Basketball League, which was a misnomer. It wasn't a league at all, really;

rather, it was a weekly practice session for boys in second through sixth grades. The elementary school basketball program had long been cut from the budget, and there was no Boys and Girls Club or YMCA or anything similar in Milan. The schools had the only gyms in town.

Josh started the league in response to the elementary school program cut, but also to emphasize fundamentals. His annual letter to every boy at Milan Elementary School also aimed to build the type of community Josh was hoping for, one centered around the goal of becoming a varsity basketball player one day. It was full of platitudes—*we have made great strides* and *all of our commitments must grow and increase if we are to have the best team and program in Indiana*—which made it all seem a bit over the heads of the Velcro-shoed set.

The practice started with almost eighty boys spread out across the gym floor in rows and columns. First, Josh stood in front of them and showed them how to get in a defensive stance—butt down, hands up, feet shoulder-width apart, knees bent, weight on the balls of their feet. Few boys got this right on the first try. Some were over-eager, their rears almost touching the floor or their weight on their toes rather than on the balls of their feet. Some just didn't seem to be trying, standing straight up with their hands out as if expecting a hug from a Disney character or a sports mascot. The coaches—Josh and Stutler, along with some volunteers from the community—did their best to correct the boys' stances, moving their hands to the right places, asking the boys to mirror them, but at times it looked like an impossible task. These boys, if they played at all, were used to shooting baskets after a varsity game. A defensive stance seemed to them an afterthought. In these eight-year-olds' minds, finding a way to put an orange ball in an orange hoop was the ultimate goal of the game.

After the coaches attempted to correct everyone's stance, it was time to get them moving in it. Josh called out that they would be sliding left three spaces, then right three spaces. "Which way is left?" Josh yelled, in a voice straight from Sesame Street. Most boys pointed left. "Okay, let's move." The boys performed the basketball version of the electric slide, first left, then right.

After about ten minutes of defensive slides, each grade went to a different basket around the gym. At one basket, Coach Day—one of the football coaches and the father of a second-grader—put the boys through a shooting regimen focused on keeping their elbows in and following through. The boys all had different ideas of what made a good shot, some shooting with two hands, some pushing the ball toward the basket from their chest like a pass. Each boy seemed comfortable sticking with what had once worked for him, and none were strong enough to shoot the ball properly: off hand barely touching the ball, primary hand cupped behind the ball with elbow flexed, jumping straight up rather than heaving the ball toward the basket, jumping their hardest toward the basket. It promised to be a long, frustrating night for both the coaches and the players.

Josh tried his best to go around to each station—ball handling, passing, pivoting drills—but after an hour he was frustrated and tired. He had been at the school since six that morning, and the caged clock on the wall showed that he had been inside Milan High School for thirteen hours. The high school practice before the youth practice had been equally frustrating, since many of the starting varsity players—Kurtis Kimla, last year's leading scorer; Zack Lewis, the starting point guard; and Alex Layden, the senior who would challenge for the point guard spot—were still held out of practice, since they were on the football team. The football team had finished the regular season with a 5–4 record but were hitting their stride in the tournament and were set to play for the sectional final that Friday. Of course, Josh wanted to see them go far in the tournament—not only would it be a great thing for the community, but he also wanted the basketball players on the team to experience what it was like to win. Still, he wanted all his players to be at practice and to get ready for the upcoming season.

The basketball jamboree—a practice tournament in which local teams would play the equivalent of a full game by playing different teams each quarter—was coming quickly, set for November 20, less than three weeks away. Without the two point guards, the team found it hard to practice their offensive plays, hard to see just how well some plays would work. Josh leaned back in the bleachers, watching nine-year-olds fail miserably in a layup drill. It was hard to know what would be easier—teaching undeveloped boys to shoot at a ten-foot goal or getting his team ready to host Hauser High School on November 23. If Josh could just get both sets of boys in the gym and never let them leave, then maybe he could turn them into a team to be reckoned with in their own time.

I was becoming frustrated too. This was not the familiar narrative. It's not what I heard each March when a midmajor Cinderella beat a major conference team. It's not what I was reminded of when a twelve seed had a five seed on the ropes. It's not what I read in articles pining for the good old days of single-class Indiana high school basketball. And, perhaps most importantly to me, it wasn't a story I wanted for my home state. Kurt Vonnegut, my favorite writer and a fellow Hoosier, once said, "I don't know what it is about Hoosiers, but wherever you go there is always a Hoosier doing something very important there." Of course, this is the same man who created the term "granfalloons" to describe a group of people (Hoosiers may be an example) who think they are connected, but turn out to only be connected through fabricated means. Their shared identity, when you get down to it, has very little meaning. While I love Vonnegut, I choose to have a rosier view of my associations with fellow Hoosiers. In Pennsylvania, I found myself surrounded by people from the dreaded East Coast—nice enough folks, but I could never seem to feel a connection with them. They were too cold, too forward. Too willing to disassociate themselves from anything that seemed to be mainstream, like basketball. For a Hoosier to separate him- or herself from basketball seemed unthinkable to me. Even Vonnegut agreed: "A Hoosier talks basketball for an hour after he is dead and has stopped breathing." Basketball connects us.

But, I wondered, what does it mean if our most important basketball story—our basketball parable, our identity—is a lie? Not that it wasn't once true: those decaying banners were proof of its existence. No blind faith needed; Milan was the David in every Hoosier. But what if Goliath had its revenge? What if David no longer lived here?

I needed to return to the movie. I was losing faith. So I visited Linda White Baurley at the Milan '54 Hoosiers Museum.

Linda White Baurley probably shouldn't care as much as she does. She's spent two years in the Milan '54 Museum as a part-time curator, giving the museum's founder, Roselyn McKittrick, time to run the antique store she owns on the other side of Milan's tiny downtown. Linda is there because she remembers all the good times of Milan—inseparable from the 1954 state championship team, which featured her brother, Gene White.

Everything about the '54 Museum is separate from the new Milan. The museum sits in the downtown that people don't visit anymore, that people have no reason to visit. The old Victorian homes aren't the kind people move into and keep up anymore; they're the kind that are split into four apartments, and the driveways are filled with seventies-era cars on blocks rather than basketball hoops, as they were in the fifties. Once, Milan's downtown featured a large hotel and spa, a drugstore, many churches, a doctor's office, a barbershop. Most no longer exist in their former roles—one storefront on Carr Street is now a public assistance office, and an old furniture store is now McKittrick's antique store, filled to the second-floor loft rafters with tin cans, bric-a-brac featuring swans and sheep, metal signs for Sinclair gas stations with their iconic dinosaur. The barbershop is now the '54 Museum, although the original mirrors and barber chairs are still in the middle of the room. The barbershop, if you removed all of the basketball memorabilia, looks exactly like the one in the movie *Hoosiers*, where the men of the community met with the new coach, Norman Dale, before the start of the season, telling him exactly how Hickory plays ball—zone defense only, and an offense focused on the quantity of shots rather than the quality.

Linda came from a basketball family. Her mother, Genevieve Ridnor, played for the Milan girls' team in 1933 and encouraged both Linda and Gene to play when they were children. By the fifties, though, the way people thought about girls' basketball had regressed into its own separate game. The game was six on six, with two girls limited to the offensive half of the court, two limited to the defensive half of the court, and two "rovers" who could run up and down the court. The game, to Linda, had become more demure and restrictive—a shadow of the game her brother Gene was allowed to play. She had no interest in this other game and devoted her basketball energies to cheering Gene on.

Her chance to cheer for Gene was nearly taken away. One night, Genevieve went to pick Gene up from his seventh-grade practice, arriving early, as she often did, to sit and watch the boys play the game she loved. At the end of the practice, she told Gene to go wait in the car. Genevieve walked up to Coach Marcus Combs, who would become the assistant for the 1954 team, and poked him in the chest.

"I want you to cut Gene," she said. Coach Combs chuckled. "I'm serious, Mr. Combs. He's slow. He's fat. He's not going to make it."

Coach Combs didn't cut Gene White from the team, and Gene did "make it." In the 1953–54 school year, Milan High School had an enrollment of 161 students, 73 of whom were boys. Fifty-eight of those boys tried out for the basketball team that fall, and Gene was one of the ten who made the team.

If it weren't for that team in 1954, there might not be anything in downtown Milan at all. But inside the small barbershop housing the '54 Museum, there's enough stuff to keep Linda White Baurley busy. Leaning against the wall under the barber's mirror sits the chalkboard that head coach Marvin Wood used to draw up the final play in the state championship game, the chalk markings preserved on the green slate. Framed pictures hang on the walls—everything from team photos to action shots to pictures of the postgame parade through downtown Milan. Blond boys with crew cuts hang out of the sides of an old school bus, waving, smiling smiles full of teeth. People in black cardigan sweaters with gold Ms on their chests wave from their front yards. In a 1995 interview, Bobby Plump—the basis for Jimmy Chitwood's character in *Hoosiers*—said of the fuss: "In Milan, people didn't look at us as if we were something special. We were just part of the community. The only way I knew we were special was when the motorcycle policeman revved up his motorcycle and took us through all those red lights."

That kind of humility is part of the 1954 story. After all, it's not like Milan hadn't experienced other successes in the fifties. The previous year, 1953, the Milan basketball team made it all the way to the championship game, losing to South Bend Central. And Milan was a successful town in other ways. The downtown hotel and spa drew visitors from nearby Cincinnati and Indianapolis, and it was still possible to make a good living on a family farm. In 1954 Milan resident Cecilia Dennis won the Miss Indiana pageant. Nineteen fifty-four, Milan's centennial, promised to be a very good year.

And yet, all of the success enjoyed by those in Milan didn't cause the type of drama usually associated with success. By all accounts, everyone in town kept a level head about the state championship, Miss Indiana, and financial prosperity. The basketball team found success because they worked at it, hard, every day. The people of Milan told themselves this story: work hard, be disciplined, and success will come.

The hard work began for the Milan team in the nearby burg of Pierceville, population forty-five. That's where Bobby Plump, Glen Butte, and Roger Schroeder played on a hoop in the alley behind Roger's parents' store, earning them the nickname "the Pierceville Alleycats." The Alleycats didn't call fouls, and a manure pile took up part of the left side of the court. When it snowed, the Alleycats put sawdust down for traction. When their hands cracked from the cold, they taped their fingers. When someone was pushed into the manure pile, the result of a hard foul, the defender held his breath a little when he guarded that kid. The boys played after school, ate dinner, and came back out until the sun went down. They made themselves ball players by repetition. At first, I wondered if today's Milan players just had too many options. Video games. Facebook. But then I remembered that many of them didn't have in-home internet, and some couldn't afford video games. Plus, if too many distractions were to blame for Milan's decline, why hadn't that affected everyone else?

The part of the '54 Museum that includes the players' input—what went in the original wood lockers the team used—is similarly boring. Each locker has the same collection of things: a letter jacket, a picture of the player back in 1954, a more recent family photo. Ron Truitt, the only deceased member of the team, was a school administrator. His locker has a picture of Truitt Middle School in the Houston suburbs, named for him after he died from cancer at age fifty-two. The outsider of the group and a film actor, Bill Jordan, has a glossy framed photo signed briskly as if for yet another adoring fan. Jordan didn't play much and preferred to go home and practice piano after school rather than play pickup basketball.

This was not exactly the stuff of literature or the movies. There simply wasn't enough tension in 1950s Milan. Angelo Pizzo wrote the *Hoosiers* screenplay because he and his college roommate at Indiana University—the director, David Anspaugh—wanted to make a movie about how important basketball was to the people of Indiana. The movie then had to be fictionalized, had to be set in the fictional Hickory and not Milan, had to have an alcoholic assistant coach and an embattled new outsider coach because, as Pizzo said, "the guys were too nice, the team had no real conflict." The reality wasn't like *Hoosiers:* the new coach didn't get fired from his last job for punching one of his players, and the old coach didn't die. Coach Marvin Wood was a quiet, married twenty-six-year-old. He replaced Herman "Snort" Grinstead, who was fired for not consulting with the superintendent before he bought new team jerseys. Despite all of the success for the small town halfway between Indianapolis and Cincinnati, Pizzo said, "their lives were not dramatic enough."

Perhaps that's why Linda, in her two years working at the '54 Museum (just a five-minute walk from Milan High School), can't recall any current player stopping in to see the museum. "It usually takes them a few years," Linda said. "Once they move away for college or work and someone outside of Milan knows about the team, they realize just how special it is."

The varsity team needed to play a game. Badly. It was only the fifth official practice of the season, just November 10, but playing against themselves had already become both boring and full of drama. During a rebounding drill, a freshman got in the face of a junior who had boxed him out a little too roughly. The junior stared into the freshman's eyes—just six inches from his—and gave him a dismissive look. "Really?" the junior asked, implying that freshmen should feel prepared to take some lumps during practice and keep their mouths shut.

One freshman who wasn't taking his lumps was Logan Alloway. The team was going through a lot of drills with small-sided teams—because what use would playing five on five be without the team's two point guards at practice? The format gave Logan more room to work, more touches on the ball. Derek Hornberger, a senior whom Josh considered cutting because he wouldn't play much (but decided against it because Derek "loved being around the team so much"), guarded Logan during one drill, and despite the size and strength difference between the two (Derek was six-feet-one and had a rugged, farmboy muscularity to him), Logan had his way with Derek. Derek tried pushing Logan around, but Logan would just speed past him. When Derek backed off and counted on his size to prevent Logan's outside shooting, Logan would put up a quick three. And during a three-on-three rebounding drill, Logan was too quick for Derek to box out, stealing some offensive rebounds from positions he shouldn't have been able to rebound from.

Halfway through the drill, Josh threw the ball at the basket to start the drill and provide a rebound for the boys to get after. Since Josh was trying to miss the shot, he threw an overhand line drive at the basket. The ball stuck between the rim and the backboard, stopping the boys in their tracks. They looked at each other. It would usually be Kurtis Kimla's job to retrieve the ball—he was the only player on the team who could dunk. But he was a football player, so he couldn't practice. Nick Ryan and Nick Walter, the tallest players on the court, looked at each other. They weren't going to try and embarrass themselves, because they knew they couldn't jump high enough to swat the ball with enough force to get it unstuck. Finally, Logan Alloway started a sprint from the perimeter, jumped at the net from a couple of yards away, and hung on the net. From the net, he pulled himself up on the rim, and—hanging by one hand—poked the ball out.

Josh looked over at Jeff and Tyler and shook his head, covering his face with his hand. The Hauser game was only two weeks away, and Hauser featured a front line of six-six, six-four, and six-three. Sixty years ago those size discrepancies wouldn't have been a problem. The myth of that team, though, had started to become a distant memory despite the banners and the museum and all of the other 1954 rhetoric. The banners hung on the wall, but they were falling apart. One day they'd be too deteriorated to read.

3

WE ASK FOR A CHANCE THAT'S FAIR

Preseason: 0–0

Kurtis Kimla walked into Josh's office on the morning of Monday, November 14, just thirty-six hours after the football team lost 28–7 in the regional finals to Guerin Catholic, a new school on the affluent north side of Indianapolis. "I'm ready to play," Kurtis said in his soft, deliberate tone. Josh smiled. Usually Kurtis's problem was that he wasn't eager enough, didn't play with enough intensity. Last year, Kurtis lead the team in scoring as a sophomore and was also a leading rebounder despite being only six feet tall. Kurtis, Zack Lewis, and John Herzog were Milan's best athletes—none of them skilled shooters, but explosive, often the fastest players on the court. Kurtis was one of the few players on the team who showed any signs of building muscle mass—his calves were larger than many of the other players' quadriceps. Kurtis was the kind of player Josh needed in order to do battle with the taller teams on the schedule.

"I know you're ready to play," Josh said, though he wouldn't have been sure if Kurtis hadn't spoken first. Zack Lewis? Josh knew he was ready to play. Zack was a competitor. Alex Layden? Josh knew he was ready to play. Zack's mom and Alex's mom were engaged in a lighthearted rivalry when Josh was around, each one teasing him about making her son the starting point guard for the year. Josh was eager to get those two on the court, to infuse some leadership and competitiveness into practice. Alex and Zack were ready too, both sending texts to Josh the day after they lost to Guerin Catholic.

And then there were the Voss boys. Most considered the Vosses the first family of Milan basketball. From the moment they could hold conversations, Ethan Voss, Braden Voss, and their cousin Alex Layden were told about the game and about the team. Their grandfather, Papaw Hank, had installed a basketball goal at one end of the concrete slab behind his house, where he parked his Milan School Corporation bus. The Voss men spent weekends and summer nights teaching Ethan, Braden, and Alex what it took to be a Milan basketball player. When the boys reached grade school, they would sometimes forego a car ride home with their moms to ride the bus with Papaw Hank. When his grandsons were on the bus, Papaw Hank knew he wasn't parking on the concrete slab out back. He also knew that he'd have to leave the porch light on for them.

Ethan had put in his time at the Marvin Wood Gym (named after the coach who led Milan to their state championship) at the middle school, put in his time at the Batesville YMCA, put in his time sitting next to his brother Braden and cousin Alex in the bleachers watching Milan team after Milan team lose. At holidays or on weekends when he'd see his family, his dad and uncles would talk about the glory days of Milan basketball, back when his uncle David Voss played. The family joked about David being "Mr. Ripley County" back then and in college, playing an extra in the movie *Hoosiers.*

Brian—Ethan and Braden's dad—and Brad were good players in their own right. Alex's mom, Anne Marie, cheered for them in high school. Even when Ethan, Braden, and Alex stepped off the court, even when they were six or eight or ten, Milan basketball was all around them. They would watch the modern-day team struggle, then go home and hear about the rich history of the program. To their credit, it didn't discourage them. It made them hungry to be the ones to return Milan to the glory they heard so much about, the glory the town expected despite the past decade or two. If Milan was a parable for boys around the country—the message of *Hoosiers* that it didn't matter where you came from or how big you were: if you worked hard and as a team, you couldn't lose—then Ethan, Braden, and Alex pictured themselves as the next chapter to the story, not another group of boys who failed to make waves of their own.

The Voss boys always seemed to have basketball on the brain, unlike Kurtis Kimla, whose commitment to the sport Josh sometimes questioned.

"You know you can't play right away," Josh said to Kurtis in his office. The Indiana High School Athletic Association's rules were clear on the matter, and they were rules Josh intended to follow. Students couldn't switch sports right away—they had to have three school days of rest before joining the next season's team for practice. "Go watch TV or something. Find a girlfriend. Do your homework." Josh grinned. He had all the time in the world now, it seemed. What would have been the first game of the season, against Hauser on November 23—just eight days away—had been postponed until December 21. Even the second game, against North Decatur, was pushed back, since Milan wouldn't be able to practice with a full team until November 18. Milan would now open the season at Lawrenceburg on December 4.

Lawrenceburg—the little town on the river—had changed quite a bit in the previous twelve years. It has always been bigger than Milan, thanks to its position directly on the Ohio River and the benefit of an exit off Interstate 275, the looped highway connecting the north side of Cincinnati to Indiana and northern Kentucky. For years, Lawrenceburg's air has been thick with the smell of booze and coal, the major industries in Dearborn County. Home to a seventy-eight-acre distillery (once owned by Seagram's, but purchased and renamed Lawrenceburg Distillers Indiana in 2007), Lawrenceburg is the perfect site for distilling—right in the middle of Indiana corn country and sitting atop an aquifer filled with naturally cold and filtered water. As the corn ferments in its mash, it fills the whole town with the sickly sweet smell of corn.

Even that might be preferred to the smell coming from the sixty-seventh dirtiest power plant in the country (based on sulfur dioxide emissions), Tanner's Creek Generating Station. One of two coal power plants near Lawrenceburg, Tanner's Creek emits a steady signal of grayish-white smoke from the Ohio River. Although Lawrenceburg was a small town in 1990, with a population of around four thousand, it was still more than double the size of Milan and seemed absolutely industrial-metropolitan by comparison. Lawrenceburg used to be the place where Milan residents would drive to visit the Walmart, a drugstore, fast-food restaurants, and casual-dining restaurants on Friday or Saturday nights. It even had the nearest movie theater. Lawrenceburg was right on an interstate and U.S. Highway 50. Milan had a four-way stop sign at the crossroads of Indiana 350 and Indiana 101.

In 1998 the gulf between Milan and Lawrenceburg widened. Argosy Casino, part of the new wave of Indiana-based riverboat casinos, opened in May. Bars, nicer restaurants, and even more McDonald's franchises popped up around the boat's permanent dock on the Ohio River, as did Holiday Inns and other nice but economy hotels. Tourism dollars and tax revenues. Lawrenceburg High School received a makeover—as a result of an influx of both tax dollars and new students. Lawrenceburg now had a Dunkin' Donuts, for Chrissake. The town felt downright suburban.

On the other hand, it was hard to tell the difference between 1998 Milan and the 2010 edition. The Jay-C Food Store (part of the low-cost Kroger chain) was still the place to get groceries. A Dairy Queen had moved in on the south side, becoming the only drive-thru in town. And Osgood—a town with about two hundred fewer people than Milan to the west—had recently opened a branch of its public library in Milan just north of The Reservation, a diner with a small teepee in its parking lot at the crossroads of State Roads 101 and 350 that was a longtime favorite of both local residents and hunters in the area during deer season. The major businesses visible in Milan were still car lots, mostly used: Milan Auto Sales, Whitewater Auto Sales, and Doug's Cars, along with a small Chevrolet dealership mostly specializing in heavy-duty trucks—Tom Tepe Autocenter—on the east side of town. Milan had stayed mostly the same size—few people moved out of town, but few moved in.

Josh and Jill Blankinship had moved to the area in the summer of 2009, but not into the town of Milan—they'd settled thirty-five minutes away in Lake Santee. Jill was in her early thirties, and she'd waited through Josh's low-paying assistant jobs before having kids. But now, culturally, Jill was on the outside. Most people in rural Indiana just didn't wait that long to start a family. She—they—wanted a child. And Josh had a head coach job now. While that offered a bit more for Josh's career and their life, Jill knew that the upcoming basketball season would put conception lower on their priority list. Still, it was another thing on Josh's mind as he geared up for the 2010–11 season.

At practice, it seemed like Ethan Voss was running the show. Since Alex Layden wasn't able to practice due to the dead period in between football and basketball seasons, Ethan and Derek Hornberger were the only seniors. Ethan was clearly more of a leader than Derek. While Ethan wasn't vocal in practice, he carried himself with a quiet but confident gait, the walk of someone who had been to thousands of basketball practices. Derek was usually more interested in flirting with the team manager, Mary-Kate Jackson. He would wipe the sweat off his head with a towel and throw it at her face, or toss his water bottle back at her so that when she caught it she squirted herself with water.

The practice was a bit of a mess. Josh had to leave school early and skip practice because his wife had gone to the emergency room complaining that she couldn't see correctly all of a sudden. (As it turned out, Jill had experienced her first migraine.) Without Josh, the gym was quieter. Coach Stutler had been a part of basketball practices in the Milan Senior High School gym since he played in the seventies, but he looked at the practice plan and asked Ethan to walk him through one of the drills he didn't remember. As practice wore on, Stutler attempted to fill the gym with the familiar boom of a coach's voice, but the yelling was hollow, devoid of motivation. Stutler would yell, "Logan, if you don't get on the floor for a loose ball . . ." and trail off, not wanting to promise punishment. He wasn't used to it; it was Josh's job.

The lack of varsity point guards also meant that there was no one on the team good enough to guard Logan Alloway at practice. While several upperclassmen struggled to shoot from the outside, Logan was already as good as Braden and Ethan Voss, already as assured. Josh had given Braden and Ethan the green light when it came to shooting open three-pointers. Logan's shooting was just as refined, the same quiet and smooth motion—his elbow at a ninety-degree angle, perpendicular to the floor instead of bowed out. Shooting coaches (of which there can be many in a town like Milan) tell players to pretend that they're shooting in a telephone booth because an elbow out to the side can cause sidespin on the ball, while an elbow tucked in assures that if the shooter's feet are set and aimed at the basket correctly, the ball will be at least on line to go in. Usually, though, this motion is difficult for young players because it means that the upper body's role is one of finesse rather than the source of power for the shot. This shooting motion relies on the lower body—the shooter jumping straight up—providing most of the power to get the ball to the basket.

It was strange that Logan, given his refined shooting style, was so accurate from distance. He was a shade above five feet eight and looked like a normal fourteen-year-old, which is to say scrawny. When he wore cutoff T-shirts to practice, when he raised his arms to shoot the ball, his ribs seemed to make cartoonish ripples down the side of his torso. But somehow, either from hours of daily practice or pure native talent, Logan's legs were strong enough for a perfect shooting stroke, one that produced high-arching, precise shots that snapped at the inside of the net with the force of their backspin.

Ten days later, the team was complete and preparing for the Lawrenceburg game in exactly one week's time. The arrival of the football players—Alex Layden, Zack Lewis, and Kurtis Kimla—had injected a bit of life into practices. The team was tired of practicing against itself, tired of fighting (and fouling) each other for rebounds in drills meant to build toughness, tired of pretending reserve players were good enough to stand in for Alex, Zack, and Kurtis. Having them in practice was like having a whole new team to play, which was exactly what Milan needed: someone else to play against, beat up on, maybe even beat.

The football players were rusty, and if they had been a new team to play, the players who had been practicing for over a month now would have little trouble beating them. Unfortunately for everyone, including Josh, who had developed a move of his own during practice—hands thrown in the air, head tilted back, asking someone to please make his boys basketball players again—the football players were on this team.

Josh had either seen enough or planned practice knowing that he'd have seen enough that early on Saturday morning. The evening before, in the post-practice huddle, most of the boys tried to joke with him, saying practice was canceled because that Saturday was the last day of deer season in Indiana. "Practice isn't until 10, guys," Josh said. "Get out there early, like you're supposed to. Plus, fishing's the only real outdoors sport. Go fishing." Maybe Josh knew his players' minds would be in the woods, focused on sighting the last buck of fall, but he planned practice in such a way that the team would end on a walkthrough of plays, so they could hopefully run them at full speed during the next week's practice. Because whatever happened that week in practice, something was bound to happen at full speed on Saturday over in Lawrenceburg's gym.

The walkthrough is where Alex Layden shined. Alex, on his way to DePauw University next fall, knew all of the plays but sometimes had trouble executing them at full speed. He was one of the smartest players on the team, but that didn't always show through in his play. Still, only a week into practice, Alex was taunting the other players with his preparedness—this after coming off of football and memorizing all his wide receiver routes and blocking assignments. "UConn!" Alex shouted out from the top of the key. "Remember UConn?"

Alex directed the boys through UConn, and once they felt comfortable with the play they ran it at close to full speed. Twenty seconds into the play, the ball was kicked out to Alex at the three-point line, with no one guarding him. Alex looked down and shuffled his feet a bit, positioning them to shoot after he received the ball, not before, the way Ethan or Logan did. Flush with confidence, Alex heaved a shot at the rim, and it landed exactly there, bouncing up and over the backboard. Josh threw his hands up and sat down on the bleachers. He was taking pieces of a team—some good, some bad, but always the positive and the negative at the same time—over to Lawrenceburg in a week.

After the boys and the managers and the balls and the jerseys and the coaches were all settled on Milan bus #41, Nancy fired up the engine and pointed its hognose front east on State Road 350. State Road 350 was a bypass of U.S. 50 (though not really a bypass in the traditional sense, to alleviate traffic buildup), giving Milan some steady connector to a bigger town, especially for the winter months. State Road 350 wasn't a straight shot to Aurora, the town right next to Lawrenceburg; rather, it rose and fell with the southern Indiana hills, wound through the ancient farmlands of eastern Ripley County and western Dearborn County, and ended at South Dearborn High School in Aurora. As the bus climbed 350 into Moore's Hill—a smattering of houses and a Sunoco station midway from Milan to Aurora—Josh shook his head and looked at Jeff.

"I can't believe he did that," Josh said, referring to Moore's Hill resident Logan Alloway. Milan's best hope for the future decided to cut class that week, and he was suspended for his first high school game. Logan wasn't on the varsity team yet, but Josh, Jeff, and Tyler all knew he would be later in the season. He had too much talent to not be useful at some point in the season, and the experience would be come in handy in the coming years, when he'd most likely be the varsity team's most important player. Jeff sat back in his seat.

"Dumbass," Jeff said.

"I mean, cutting class? Really?" Josh said, rubbing his forehead quickly in frustration. "Every teacher takes attendance on the computer now. They know when you've come to school but not to their class."

"Dumbass," Jeff repeated, with the same pace and intonation. As the JV coach, Jeff was looking forward to having a scoring option that no one in Lawrenceburg knew about yet. Sure, some of the neighboring schools—Jac-Cen-Del, Batesville, South Ripley—knew Milan had Logan, mostly because all of those kids played together at the YMCA in Batesville from time to time. But Lawrenceburg would probably have no clue.

"Still a kid, I guess," Josh said, trying to get his six-foot-four frame comfortable in the front seat of the school bus. They stayed quiet for the rest of the trip.

Anxiety and the expression of anxiety can take many forms, and when boys are in a gym in Indiana on an icy late afternoon in early December, far before game time, anxiety turns to action. The JV game wouldn't start until 6 p.m., but Nancy's bus pulled in next to the redbrick Lawrenceburg High School at 4:30. The team and managers followed Josh and the assistant coaches through a hallway and down some stairs into the gym. The visitors' locker room was small, barely big enough for the JV team, let alone both the JV and the varsity. The bottleneck of coaches and managers and players caused half the team—

the half in the back of the bus, the varsity—to wait outside the locker room for a few minutes. Someone in Lawrenceburg had just turned on the gym's game lights—round fluorescent floodlights with cages over their metal fixtures.

Kurtis Kimla grabbed a ball from the bag outside the locker room and threw it to Braden Voss. He picked out one for himself and jogged onto Lawrenceburg's orange-and-black-lined court. Kurtis bounced the ball, noticing the way the game lights hit the glossy sealant on the floor. This wasn't the Milan gym at 10 a.m. on a Saturday; it wasn't rebounding drills and endless amounts of free throws. This was the first game of the season.

Kurtis looked around at Lawrenceburg's gym, the seating rounded at the edges on one end of the court, which gave the floor a sunken-in feeling. Then, standing in the corner of the court, Kurtis looked at the rim, took a couple of dribbles in place, and started a sprint toward the goal, cupping the ball in his right hand and jumping off of his left foot when he reached the edge of the lane. He extended the ball toward the rim, and it clanged off of the back of the rim, arching toward those game lights. Kurtis hung on the rim, bending the breakaway goal straight down toward the floor as the ball flew back over him, falling near where he jumped from. Kurtis took a second to hang on the rim and smile at his teammates. He didn't make the dunk, but it didn't matter. He was attempting a dunk on a court other than Milan's, and they were about to play a team whose jerseys weren't gold or black or simply the pale peach of a Milan player's skin. The season was here, the weather was turning cold, and they had access to a foreign gym with nothing but the game lights on for a good forty-five minutes. It was a good night to be sixteen years old in Indiana, and Kurtis—his teammates eventually joining in but not coming very close—continued to attempt to dunk.

Inside the locker room, with a moment to himself, Josh took his long-sleeved gold Milan shooting shirt off. He slapped his stomach—fat by no means but starting to show the bulk and slowed metabolism of a twenty-eight-year-old man. Or maybe of a man who wakes up at 5:30 a.m. most mornings to drive thirty-five minutes to Milan to let someone into the gym, or to plan for his PE class because he didn't get a chance in between planning for varsity practice and setting up the Milan Youth Basketball League, and because of that, a man who doesn't have time to pack his lunch and either has to walk across the street to the Jay-C Food Store and buy a bag of Chex Mix for lunch (and usually dinner) or drive down to the Dairy Queen and have a cheeseburger. Or maybe after practice at 8:30, he'd stop at Taco Bell, the one at the Batesville exit on Interstate 74 on his way home to Lake Santee.

Due to that schedule or a nervous habit, in his most anxious moments—like the hour leading up to the first JV and varsity games of the season—Josh shaved. He didn't have much to shave—the blond facial hair that matched his closely cropped buzz cut was barely noticeable and patchy—but the process seemed to soothe him. Josh leaned over the visitors' locker room sink, wearing black jogging pants and white socks, and looked in the mirror. Spreading shaving cream on his face, Josh didn't think about the fact that his team knew about four plays, and not well. Pulling the plastic disposable razor down from his sideburns, Josh didn't consider that Milan hadn't won the first game of the season in eight years, didn't consider the ten years that had passed since Milan beat Lawrence-burg in the regular season. Wiping his face with a towel, Josh wasn't thinking about three of his most important players having just two weeks of practice to switch from football to basketball. Josh had been thinking about those things all week, and once he put his Milan basketball golf shirt on and affixed to its lapel the guardian angel pin his wife Jill bought for him that week, he'd start to think about them again. But for that moment, he didn't feel the pressure of coaching those twenty boys—he was just a young man shaving in a high school locker room.

When the JV team walked into the locker room following their loss, Josh was sitting there with the varsity team. He had promised himself that he wouldn't watch much of the JV games this year, because last year—in his first year as a head coach—the games made him so furious that he was too wound up to properly coach the varsity team. Of course, he knew it was a promise that he wouldn't keep. For one thing, he had to know how his JV players were playing in case some of the varsity players got hurt and he needed to call someone up to varsity. Plus, he would be coaching the JV players in just a few years. Some of them would likely be on the varsity team next year, or even make the sectional roster. Josh had caught bits of the game from the corner of the gym, where the gap between the bleacher seats formed a tunnel leading from the visitors' locker room to the gym. He saw enough of the game to know what went wrong.

"Well, someone let you down tonight, boys," Josh said, ignoring whatever Coach Stutler might have prepared to tell his team. "And I know you're all buddies, and you're all young, but you better grow up a little bit. You better grow up as a team. It starts in practice, and it starts in the classroom."

As Josh returned to the varsity locker room, Alex Layden was motioning for everyone to huddle up. The team draped their arms around each other's shoulders, their gold shooting shirts pulling tight across their chests as they raised their arms, stretching the white embroidered "MILAN" from side to side. Alex, with his arms around his cousins Ethan and Braden, leaned his head into the middle of the huddle as the boys swayed their shoulders side to side, keeping their feet planted. No one told them to sway, just as no one told them to repeat after Alex—it was as if this were as natural as brushing their teeth before bed.

Alex looked each of his teammates in the eye, ending with Braden and Ethan. After he spoke, the team repeated after him, the urgency in their voices increasing with every line, until their shouts echoed off the lockers.

Dear Lord, the battles we go through in life:
we ask for a chance that's fair.
A chance to equal our stride
a chance to do or dare.
If we should win
let it be by the code,
faith and honor held high.
If we should lose,
we'll stand by the road
and cheer as the winners go by.
Day by day,
get better and better,
till we can't be beat,
won't be beat!

4

HOME

The First Game: 0–0

Afer Tyler turned to Josh and told him about the goosebumps he had after the team's cheer, and after Josh nodded in agreement, they couldn't help but feel a little corny. Since Lawrenceburg was only ten or fifteen minutes from Milan, Josh and Tyler expected a big crowd from both schools. However, when the boys walked out onto the court and looked up at the stands in the 2,700-capacity gym, they were only a quarter full. Only about seventy-five of those fans were wearing the black and gold of Milan.

Tyler poked Josh with his elbow as they walked toward the bench. "School spirit is going down the tubes," he said to Josh. The departure of school spirit must have been a recent and abrupt phenomenon, since Tyler and Josh were only two and eleven years removed from playing high school basketball.

As the Lawrenceburg Tigers jogged onto the court, and as the band played the school fight song, the Lawrenceburg cheerleaders stood in front of the student section. All of the cheerleaders clapped along to the fight song, but after the first couple of lines it was clear that many of them didn't know the words.

So instead of mumbling what they thought were the words or the old "just say watermelon" trick, several girls started talking to their friends in the front row.

Josh leaned over to Tyler and spoke above the band. "What else are these kids doing on a Friday night?" he asked.

If there was something more important to do on Friday night, the members of the Milan basketball team had no idea what that would be. While the team waited on the bench for the starting lineup to be announced, Mary-Kate and Vicky were busy handing out towels. Every player wanted one, and they hadn't even run up and down the court yet. As Josh kneeled in front of the team bench and gave some final instructions, each of the players sat hunched over, elbows resting on knees, gripping a towel in his sweaty hands.

In the first few minutes of the game, it seemed Ethan still needed to wipe his hands on a towel. The only starting senior for Milan was tentative, shuffling his feet when he received the ball instead of keeping them set and shooting confidently. He missed his first three-pointer of the game and on Milan's next possession decided not to shoot when he was open. As Lawrenceburg's shot at the halftime buzzer hit the rim and floated up, Josh started walking across the court. As it fell through the hoop to make the halftime score 25–19, Josh was almost underneath the basket and could have caught the ball and handed it to the official. But he had his head down, thinking of Milan's seven missed layups and eleven turnovers. The turnovers were expected: it was the first game of the season, and Lawrenceburg liked to press. Sure, eleven turnovers were a lot for one game, let alone a half. Too many turnovers was a problem that could be fixed, would probably even fix itself as the boys played in more games and the intensity of practices picked up in the middle of the season. But seven missed layups? Some of them weren't even challenged by Lawrenceburg players. Josh could remember a particularly good group of sixth-graders at Milan Youth Basketball League practice making eight layups in a row during a drill. Josh wasn't even so bothered by the number of missed layups and the fourteen points they could have represented. It was the way his players were missing them, stopping before the rim and hooking the ball over their heads or timidly jumping up. No one was driving to the basket and exploding to the backboard. Milan looked timid. They looked small.

Ethan Voss tried to be the senior leader the team needed out of halftime. He took the first two threes open to him and missed both on Milan's first possession. Josh threw his hands up in the air and looked at the empty seats behind the Milan bench. He couldn't make the open shots for them. Josh sat down and grabbed the empty Diet Mountain Dew bottle next to his seat. Holding it by the cap, he anxiously patted the end of the bottle against his left hand. He watched as Lawrenceburg missed a three that would have made the deficit twelve points—more than Milan had managed to score in a quarter—and watched as Ethan dribbled down the right side of the lane and shot another soft layup. "At least he drew contact," Josh muttered, despite the nod it drew from Coach Stutler. Ethan's first free throw was far too hard, bouncing off the back of the rim and almost back to the free throw line. His second barely scraped the front of the rim. Josh whipped the bottle against the bleacher and stomped on it. Layups. Turnovers. Missed free throws. On the next Lawrenceburg possession they managed two offensive rebounds. The boys from Milan didn't get many chances, and the ones they got they seemed to waste.

In the fourth quarter, though, Lawrenceburg began to waste their chances. Ethan made a three-pointer, cutting Lawrenceburg's lead to two. Josh pumped his fist, knowing that with six minutes left anything could happen. Lawrenceburg had let Milan in, or maybe the Milan boys felt they had clawed their way back. Either way, all that mattered was the scoreboard. A season-opening win would mean so much, would be such a rare thing for the school. Josh called off the press that had helped the team keep the game close and messy enough to let anything happen. Milan still looked small, but at least they now looked quick and scrappy.

Milan hadn't played particularly well all game, that was clear. But even after several years of poor play, Milan fans were not used to losing. In fact, Milan basketball fans normally discussed what kind of strategies would lead to a win each night. To them, it wasn't that the team needed better, bigger, stronger players, ones who could shoot more accurately or block more shots. It was just that they needed to focus on what they did best—playing within themselves, getting the Voss boys open looks. However, that talk was usually reserved for before and after games. During games, when things started going downhill, as they threatened to do the entire Lawrenceburg game, fans traded knowing glances.

So when Ethan Voss tied the score with a three-pointer to send Milan's first game into overtime, Milan's fans were excited, but the excitement seemed to come with a tone of fulfilled expectations. *Ethan Voss needs to shoot the three consistently for Milan to win,* the fans had always told themselves. *They have to play scrappy defense and use their quickness before their size is exposed.* The team had finally done what was expected of them all along.

For younger fans, the overtime was a bit more exciting. Mary-Kate Jackson, the team's manager, put towels on the shoulders of each of the boys as they sat in the huddle before overtime. Timidly, she sat down, organizing the water bottles on the floor behind her feet. "I'm about to pass out," she said to Vicky Cunningham, the other manager, as she bounced her legs up and down. Vicky rolled her eyes and checked her phone for text messages.

The confidence of the Milan fans transferred to the players in overtime. Instead of throwing the ball away, Milan drew fouls from the aggressive Lawrenceburg defense. Instead of missing low-percentage shots, Milan attempted one field goal in the overtime on which they were not fouled—a made layup by Alex Layden after a steal. Instead of leaving men open, the Milan defense forced turnovers. Lawrenceburg had three looks at game-tying three-point shots in the last twenty seconds, but none fell. For the first time in eight years, Milan won the first game of the season.

Josh jogged off the court with the boys, but instead of immediately celebrating with the team, he stood outside the locker room, leaning against the wall, bent over at the waist with his face in his hands. He looked up at Jeff, who was grinning so wide that the gaps in his smile on the sides showed. "I'm so tired," Josh said. "I can't even go nuts."

As the boys showered, Josh went into the stands and talked to Jill. She rubbed his back beneath his shoulder blades, let her newly painted fingernails scratch him through the Milan basketball shirt. Josh looked out on the court, the scene of so much nervous energy before the game and so much hard work during the game. He looked at the spot on the floor where he had stomped in frustration several times during the game, now the spot where a couple of Lawrenceburg fans sat. Josh looked at the spot on the floor where a Lawrenceburg player lost a tooth diving for a ball in overtime, now where a Lawrenceburg assistant coach swooped up his three-year-old son, giving him raspberries on his stomach. Josh watched as two Lawrenceburg grade-school boys tried to shoot from where Ethan Voss tied the game up at the end of the fourth quarter, from the elbow of the three-point line. The boys took the ball and flipped it in the air with backspin so it bounced into their hands. They weren't strong enough to shoot from the three-point line just yet, but they knew enough to practice catching the ball as if from a pass instead of working it over in their hands like they could only do with a free throw. Despite the home team's loss, the atmosphere on the court wasn't negative at all—it was just a gym where the losing assistant coach could chase his young son around the court, and young Indiana boys could dream of being Ethan Voss, even if he played for a different school. Maybe it was worth it to still believe in basketball.

Milan wanted to play North Decatur on a Saturday night, but instead— because of the football team's run in the state tournament—they were playing on Tuesday, December 7. They'd get one shot at their section's favorites during the regular season, and this year Milan got to play the Chargers at home. Despite a 16–107 record over the past six years, and only twelve wins at home, Milan usually enjoyed a good home crowd on the weekends. Milan's population was 1,899, and on a Friday or Saturday night Milan did its best to fill at least half of the 2,076-capacity gym. Sure, the basketball team hadn't had a winning season or won a tournament game since 2003–4. And the football team had enjoyed a fair amount of success and were drawing large crowds of their own. However, the success of the football team didn't overshadow the basketball team. Were there a few more Milan football T-shirts in the gym's crowd on winter nights? Yes. Even Coach Stutler wore his Milan football jacket to and from basketball games. It didn't change the fact that, against all odds, people expected to see something surprising when they went to a Milan basketball game. People always expected to see Milan perform their miracle.

When fans enter the Milan Senior High School gym, it's difficult to overlook the history of the school. To the left, they see the 1954 state championship trophy, with the net from the final game slung over it. The team picture taken after the game hangs in the gym, but the face of each player and coach has been blown up and put in its own eight-by-ten-inch frame on the wall around the trophy, with the every name engraved on a brass plate. The pictures look distorted—the boys' skin tone bleached out, with small prisms along the lines of their faces from the computer's alteration. To the right, behind the two ladies sitting at a card table selling tickets to the game for five dollars, hangs an old scoreboard. The scoreboard employs different-colored lightbulbs—red for the score, green for the time. It is plugged into the wall and has a light switch to turn it off and on to the only time and score it knows: 0:00, Home 32, Visitors 30—the final score from the 1954 state championship against Muncie Central.

Just beyond the bay of four doors leading into the gym sit enough bleachers to hold the entire town, plus another three hundred people. On the wall nearest the entrance hangs a banner that says "State Finalist 1953" and "Milan State Champs 1954." Both banners are black with gold borders and lettering, and a picture of the 1954 team is bolted to the cinder-block wall between them. Both banners have water spots from prolonged, inadequate storage, and the gold border and letters are tattered, although it's unclear what has caused the damage. Next to the banners, centered on the wall above "MHS" in gold lettering, is a painting of an Indian chief in full headdress. The chief looks out onto the court with the solemnity we've come to expect from re-creations of Indian chiefs: pursed lips, a fixed stare, a proud posture.

The floor is a light parquet, pine-colored, and the oak free throw lanes are slightly darker. At midcourt, in the jump ball circle, the same slightly darker parquet reveals the state of Indiana. In the southeast corner, a black star locates Milan. Right above the star is the word "Hysteria" in large gold letters with a white background, making the word, and the word "Hoosier" above it, seem cartoonishly flown in over the state of Indiana. Altogether, the half-court artwork reads "Heart of Hoosier Hysteria" with "Milan Indiana" below it, hugging the bottom of the circle. It's a gym you would expect something great to happen in, because it represents only the great things from the past.

In the locker room the boys tried to avoid feeling anxious about facing North Decatur. It had been seven years since Milan beat North Decatur in the sectional semifinals. But that was the 2003–4 team: the last Milan team to win a tournament game, the last Milan team to have a winning record, the last Milan team to win more than four games in a season. *Maybe things have changed,* some people in Milan started to think. They had a new head coach with a year's experience. Josh was young, only twenty-eight, only two years older than Marvin Wood was when he led the 1954 team to the state championship and earned Milan the title "The Heart of Hoosier Hysteria."

Josh had started to change things too. The Milan Youth Basketball League was a long-needed step to develop the elementary school players. Josh took the boys to D-One team camp the previous summer, a popular camp in Indiana run by Jerry Hoover, an Indiana high school coaching legend. Josh fought to get the boys in the gym over the summer and in the weight room to improve their fitness. The high school game had passed the era of the two-handed set shot and the no-contact defense. It was now a more physical game, more dependent on players executing intricate plays on offense, relying on speed and strength rather than patience and accuracy. It was a change that occurred much earlier than Josh's arrival in 2009, but one that he nonetheless had to introduce to Milan's team.

Not only had the game of basketball changed since 1954, but the culture had changed for the players as well. Before the North Decatur game, Milan's team listened to some pregame music. It was clear—clear from the way the boys responded when Braden Voss queued up the track, clear from the way they nodded their heads as if to say, *of course, this song*—that the first track played on the makeshift stereo (the boys used the DVD player and TV they watched game tape on as a CD player) would be the anthem for the upcoming season. It was "Black and Yellow," a song by the newly popular Pittsburgh rapper Wiz Khalifa. It was December 7, and some of the boys had just finished hanging their Carhartt winter coats in their lockers and storing their brown leather snow boots under the bench in front of their lockers, but buzz-cut heads bobbed as the boys mouthed explicit lyrics about making millions.

After "Black and Yellow," a techno song came on, and Nick Ryan jogged over to the light switch and made the fluorescent bulbs strobe, like a rave. Track three was "Heart of a Champion," a seven-year-old song by the rapper Nelly. During the CD's eighth track, 50 Cent's "In Da Club," Kurtis Kimla and Nick Ryan took turns guarding each other on playacted post moves. It was clear that the man with the ball was always playing the part of North Decatur's Bobby Beeler. Beeler was a bench player, but he was a six-foot-eight junior. He seemed to be a bench player only because he couldn't make it up and down the court very easily. The game tape and the scouting report had warned Nick and Kurtis—the boys who would be responsible for guarding Beeler—that his favorite move was a drop step over his left shoulder, always with an elbow into his man's sternum. For Nick and Kurtis, that elbow would be about nose-high. Kurtis and Nick were obviously worried about Beeler, but in the classic style of seventeen-year-old boys, they showed their anxiety through horseplay, by trying to prove that it was the last thing they were worried about, the first thing they were excited to see in person.

Josh was missing the mimicked defensive plan for Bobby Beeler in the locker room. He stood in front of the mirror in his private bathroom and poked his finger into a package of cotton balls, hooking his finger under the plastic and ripping a hole in the top of the bag. He removed four cotton balls and set three on the ledge of the sink. He fluffed the fourth one in his fingers, pulling the cotton apart as if it were putty, and stuffing it into his ear. He then went to work on the other cotton balls, putting two in each ear. When Josh was stressed, it meant his ears were acting up again. During the previous year he'd missed a game at the end of the season for ear surgery—he had bloody drainage filling up his ear canal. That ear fixed, his other ear had started to do the same thing. "Gotta get this figured out," he yelled out to Jeff. "I'm not going through this shit again this year."

"I've put a quote on the scouting report," Josh said to the team several minutes later. "William Shakespeare said it. It's 'Things won are done; joy's soul lies in the doing.'" *Troilus and Cressida*. A little-known Shakespearean tragedy in the middle of southeastern Indiana farmland. Cressida, the daughter of a Trojan priest who has betrayed Troy and turned to the Greeks, admires Troilus, a Greek warrior and prince who describes himself as lovesick about Cressida, to the point that it affects his performance on the battlefield. However, she knows that once she submits to Troilus, his interest will wane. At the end of act 1, scene 2, she reveals to the audience her plan to play coy with Troilus. *Things won are done*, she says, intending to keep Troilus in pursuit of her. Later, of course, as these things happen in Shakespearean tragedies, Troilus and Cressida are split apart by the Trojan War, and Cressida becomes one of Troilus's enemies' lovers.

Josh had only intended to keep the team's focus away from their opening game win. *Keep going*, Josh wanted to communicate to the boys. *Reliving the past isn't as good as continuing to win.* It was a message Milan needed to hear, with the banners and the trophies and the scoreboards all reminding them of 1954, reminding them of that glory season fifty-seven years ago. If only Josh could keep the Greeks and Trojans from tearing Troilus and Cressida apart.

The pregame culture for Milan—one dependent on the participation of fans, cheerleaders, and players—belied the fact that Milan had not been good at basketball for several years. Especially for a small school, Milan's home game routine was ordered, impressive, and perhaps intimidating for visiting teams. It relied on tradition, and tradition intimidates because it presupposes that a lot of people care. It's the reason high schools and colleges get branded as "football schools" or "basketball schools": if the football team wins and the basketball team loses, why spend money that could be spent on football tickets on seeing a perennial loser? Why paint your chest when the game won't be televised?

The year 1954 had allowed Milan to get past the lack of winning and sustain tradition, although the things that contributed to the tradition were in no way located in the 1950s. During warm-ups, the Milan pep band played Bon Jovi's "Livin' on a Prayer," to which the cheerleaders performed a line dance that would have more closely fit Brooks and Dunn's "Boot Scootin' Boogie." Dressed in long-sleeved black tops with "Milan" in gold across the chest and short black skirts with white-and-gold piping, the cheerleaders kicked their white tennis shoes as if they were cowboy boots, twirled and clapped when they were halfway there, and grapevined to *oh, oh, livin' on a prayer*. After North Decatur was introduced by Marty Layden—the PA announcer, middle school principal, and Alex Layden's father—the gym lighting was cut to total darkness. There were no gasps—not from Milan fans, and not from North Decatur fans, who must have known from previous trips to Milan what was about to happen. The band's bass drummer started in with one hard beat on the drum, followed by three softer beats—the familiar drumming of the "tomahawk chop," the cheer made popular by the Atlanta Braves during their dominance in the 1990s, and also known as Florida State University's war chant, popular from much the same era. The Milan fans, using the hands they'd just used to cover their hearts during the national anthem, chopped their hands, holding their elbow at a ninety-degree angle and then releasing it to a 180-degree angle, wailing the *Ohhhhh, oh, ohohoh, ohohoh, oh ohohoh* of the mock Indian war chant along with the brass section of the Milan High School band. A student flipped on a spotlight at the top of the home bleachers, right next to where the basketball managers had set up the camcorder to tape the game. It was Milan's version of the 1990s Chicago Bulls introduction, total darkness except for a spotlight searching the floor during the introduction of the home team. Instead of the Alan Parsons Project's "Sirius" pumping through the United Center sound system, the few hundred Milan fans—again, almost half the town's population—kept the war chant going.

Right before tipoff, two seniors at Milan High School passed out paper bags to the entire student section and to most of the adult home fans. No one looked quizzically at the bags or put them under their feet on the bleachers or said "no, thank you" to the students. The fans took the brown paper bags with a smile and blew into them as if they were hyperventilating from the exciting pregame introductions. Once the bags were filled with air, the fans held them in one hand at their side.

It would have taken an uninformed visitor exactly seventeen seconds after the tipoff to understand the value of the paper bags. After Nick Ryan batted the tip into the backcourt for Zack Lewis to retrieve, Zack dribbled up the court and passed off to John Herzog, who drove down the lane and kicked the ball out to Ethan Voss on the right wing. As Ethan's three-point shot sailed through the net, the sound of hundreds of paper bags popping created a sound like the world's largest microwave popcorn bag, its thousands of kernels all popping within seconds of each other.

The game was played at an unnaturally fast pace—Isaac Loechle, North Decatur's best player and a conference player of the year candidate, made sure of that. The guard made three straight three-pointers in the first quarter, each one from far behind the arc, and after each one he would bounce and preen a bit, then set up the North Decatur full-court press. North Decatur wanted to speed the game up because they knew Milan could be forced into quick, bad shots. And they knew that the good shots Milan got—layups—were often missed.

5

WORKING FOR FREE

December 17: 2–1

When Jeff Stutler was ejected early in the second quarter of the junior varsity game at Trinity Lutheran, Milan fans and players knew they were in for a weird night. Even though it was a Friday, the Milan players hadn't had school that day—or the previous few days—because of a snowstorm. Milan, like most rural Indiana schools, shut down easily in the winter because of the number of remote households in the district and the lack of municipal plowing service. Unless you owned a snowplow attachment for a pickup truck or lived on State Road 101 or 350, it was easy to get snowed in. Especially when teenage drivers were involved, it didn't make sense to hold school when the weather got bad.

Since the players hadn't had school, they were without the small amount of focus and discipline it provided them throughout the day. Some players, like Derek Hornberger, drove large four-wheel-drive pickup trucks and could go visit friends or girlfriends. Snowball fights popped up around town among those within walking distance. Alex, Braden, and Ethan liked to play video games all day. At least at school, the players would have had a few quiet moments to daydream about the game or read the scouting report or stop by Josh's office and watch game tape during study hall.

And yet Milan made the hour-long drive west on U.S. 50 to Seymour that Friday night. Trinity Lutheran hadn't thought to cancel the game because, in a town of around eighteen thousand, they had long ago cleaned the streets from the week's snowfall.

The environs of Trinity Lutheran didn't help focus the players either. It was a small school of just over a hundred students in grades nine through twelve. The gym, which was inside what looked like a pole barn, had a set of bleachers across from the benches but no bleachers on the other side—just one steel bench behind some folding chairs where the team managers could sit. Behind that, a yellow cinder-block wall was adorned with a large wooden back-lit cross. It looked like a gym at a church camp.

The boys from Milan, many of them with their large headphones still on from the bus ride, wearing black, white, and gold warm-ups, looked the part of a flashy city school even though it was just a desperate reach for how a city school might act. Many of the players sported earrings—Nick Ryan wore fake diamond studs; Logan Alloway wore earrings with the famous Air Jordan silhouette. Milan was in farm country, unlike Seymour, which still enjoyed some industrial and commercial economic success. Seymour still maintained a middle class. In Milan the middle class was vanishing at an alarming but unsurprising rate.

Culturally, Milan and Trinity Lutheran were very different as well. The Trinity Lutheran fans and students just seemed a little too nice. Their cheerleaders didn't chant "hey miss it, miss it" when opponents shot free throws. Their fans didn't yell at the referees. Their players didn't seem to take basketball as seriously, and their coaches seemed relaxed. For Milan, basketball was a serious enterprise, an undertaking that required players and coaches to have teeth-grinding focus and an event that caused parents and fans to be on edge during the game. There was a history to defend, even if year after year they had failed to match the success of the past. In Milan, basketball meant something even though the rewards seemed few.

The Milan players were nervous when they stepped into the gym thirty minutes before the start of the JV game. Josh had noticed them horsing around on the bus, noticed the candy wrappers flying through the air at the younger players' heads, noticed the boys huddled around Zack Lewis's phone as he texted back and forth with a girl. On the bus they were relaxed, happy. But right before they got off the bus, Josh told the team what they probably already knew and didn't want to admit: that they weren't ready to play.

As the JV game started, Josh stood against the wall in the corner of the gym opposite the Milan bench. He liked to chat with John Prifogle, the athletic director and his landlord, before games because John was not only a former Milan basketball player but also a calming influence, someone who didn't talk so much that Josh became annoyed before a game. Plus, John was personally calming to Josh. Earlier in the week, there were rumors that a small group of parents were growing restless with Josh as a coach. It wasn't the winning and losing. The Indians were 2–1 thanks to a 60–52 win over South Decatur the previous Friday, and it was the first (albeit early) winning record people in Milan could remember for a long time. Also, they had hung with the sectional favorites, North Decatur, for their only loss. Basketball-wise, things seemed to be changing for the better in the eyes of the Milan fans. But some players' parents were growing tired of Josh's tirades on the sidelines. John told Josh that he was handling it and that he hadn't seen anything to be worried about in Josh's excitement on the sidelines.

Nearly eleven months had passed since the January morning Josh opened the front door of the small house he rented from his athletic director on Lake Santee, a thirty-five-minute drive from Milan and a thirty-minute drive from Shelbyville's Major Hospital, where his wife, Jill, had found a job as a nurse, and dusted the snow off the plastic bag around the *Indianapolis Star*. Nearly eleven months since, to his surprise, he saw Milan's interim superintendent, Steve Gookins, quoted on the front page of the sports section. Nearly eleven months since he read Gookins's words—"re-evaluate what direction we're headed" and "change the culture" and "put some fun back into sports"—and paired them with the reporter's words: "In Milan, superintendent Steve Gookins has proposed taking away coaching stipends and instituting volunteer coaches, a move he said would save $210,000 of the $368,000 his district needs to slice."

The only thing that sounded good to Josh from that *Indianapolis Star* article was "put some fun back into sports." On January 25, 2010, when Josh read that his boss was considering reducing his job title to *middle school physical education teacher*, he was concerned for the other part of his job title. The Indians were 3–9 at that point in the year and had just lost to rival South Ripley 70–43. And it was true: sports weren't as much fun as they were when Josh was at powerhouse New Albany, just across the Ohio River from Louisville, Kentucky. At New Albany, he coached JV players who would one day challenge for regional titles and college scholarships.

But now he was in Milan. Josh loved the idea of taking the Milan job, loved the history of the program, saw a community who wanted to not just care about basketball, but care about winning basketball again. Milan fans were going to show up: they did it for football and did it for basketball. The adults would show up because that's what people did on a Friday or Saturday night. Students were a different story: if a team wasn't winning and if the adults were showing up only to complain, they'd just focus on football and take the winter off. But the adults would always care about the basketball tradition because it's what everyone knew about Milan. The tradition—which was really just sixty-year-old success—meant identity.

In the tradition, in the history, Josh saw stability. While Milan offered a level of prestige due to the 1954 championship and *Hoosiers,* it was also a program whose recent history was so bad that even a .250 win percentage would be a large improvement. Winning just a few games could mean job security for Josh and the chance to start a family with Jill. And here, on newsprint, with ink possibly made from the soybeans Josh had passed hundreds of times on his drive to Milan, the *Indianapolis Star* had taken away all of that security. It was the last thing he had considered when he took the Milan coaching job: that in the home of *Hoosiers,* the boys' head basketball coach job might be cut altogether. The lead of the article asked a question that Josh wasn't prepared to answer: *Would you work for free?* With his whole career ahead of him, he knew his answer would probably be no.

It was a question that Jeff Stutler was also obliged to consider eleven months before Milan's game at Trinity Lutheran in Seymour. Coaching pay was safe for the moment, if a 50 percent reduction in Josh's pay and the loss of a paid varsity assistant could be considered safe. But Jeff was forced into doing two jobs—the varsity assistant and the junior varsity head coaching positions—and he was finding it difficult to complete both. Practice time focused on the varsity team's goals and used the JV players as a scout team, with each player mimicking the opposition varsity player who most resembled him on defense. Promising young junior varsity players like Logan Alloway and Logan Karstetter were often running plays they'd never run in a varsity game in a few years.

It was easy to see how frustrated that made Jeff and his JV team. After a week of running another team's offense, sometimes it was difficult to make sure the junior varsity players knew how to run their own offense on game day. If Logan Alloway cut the wrong way on the perimeter or Logan Karstetter forgot whose man to pick on a play, Jeff would grind his teeth and sit down on the bench. Often his halftime and postgame speeches focused on instruction rather than motivation. Sure, there were times when Jeff yelled and told the team he didn't think they were working very hard or focusing—the fourteen- and fifteen-year-olds on the team *did* have a penchant for goofing off like the immature teenagers they were—but for the most part he focused on what went wrong and how to fix it next time. For the most part, Jeff kept his cool, at least outwardly.

That's why many people were shocked when Jeff Stutler was ejected from the JV game. He wasn't stomping up and down the sidelines (as Josh sometimes did), but had been given technical fouls for disagreeing with the referees in a slightly elevated voice. After his first technical, given by a gel-haired referee in his early twenties, Jeff was ordered to sit on the bench for the rest of the game— his standing privileges had been revoked. His second technical came when he said, "How was that not a foul down there?" at the same referee as he ran past during play. When the referee turned around to give the second technical, Jeff's eyes grew large. "You've got to be kidding me!" Jeff shouted, the maddest and loudest he had been all game. "That's how insecure you are as an official?"

Josh walked around the gym floor, watching Jeff and the referee continue to talk. "Buh-bye," the referee finally said, waving his hands and mimicking the David Spade flight attendant character from *Saturday Night Live*, the skit that aired when the referee was approximately six years old. Josh muttered to himself as he walked with a larger-than-normal stride to the Milan bench. He adjusted the cotton ball in his ear. Normally Josh didn't even like to watch the JV game—it irritated him too much—but now he not only had to watch the JV game but also try to get the freshmen and sophomores on the team to run Milan's plays to his standards.

Josh started to yell instructions to the JV players, who were stunned that the quiet, reserved Coach Stutler had been thrown out of a game. Varsity coaches were rarely ejected, but junior varsity coaching ejections were unheard of. Just as Josh got the boys set in the defense he wanted, the other referee jogged over. "You have to stay seated, coach. Your bench has already been warned." Josh made a show of sitting down, crossing his legs at the ankles, and folding his hands on top of his head with his elbows out as if to fake relaxation. He looked over at the Trinity Lutheran staff members working the scorers' table and chuckled, making sure they took note of how ridiculous the referees were acting. The Trinity Lutheran scorers only looked forward, a mix of embarrassment and gravity inspiring their facial expressions.

At the end of three quarters, the JV team seemed to have all of the excitement behind them. Jeff, not knowing whether he was allowed to come out of the locker room for the second half and sit in the stands or if he was going to be allowed to sit on the bench for the varsity game, stayed quiet for most of halftime. What would he have to say? It was Josh's team now. As the boys received their instructions on the bench before the start of the fourth quarter, the scoreboard read 26–20. A couple of Logan Alloway shots could tie the game in a hurry.

But a comeback wasn't to be. Even if it was to be, the JV players didn't meet fate halfway. As the team jogged off the court after being outscored 16–4 in the fourth quarter for a 42–24 final, Josh barked at Logan Alloway. The yelling continued in the locker room. Josh pointed at Logan and then at each member of the JV team. "When you guys want to grow up and run plays and actually play hard, let me know," Josh said. "I might have you guys practicing with the junior high team this week. You're no use at all to us in practice, and you showed why tonight."

While Jeff and Josh were talking to the JV team, and while the varsity team warmed up, John Prifogle was asking around about Jeff Stutler. He asked the varsity game referees, called athletic director friends, talked to the Trinity Lutheran athletic director. Finally, when the coaching staff had come out of the locker room to watch the team warm up, John had an answer. Jeff couldn't be on the bench for the varsity game. John walked around the court to the Milan bench where Jeff and Josh were sitting and gave them the news.

"That makes me look like a fuckin' idiot," Jeff said, finally showing some anger about the whole thing. "That's what you get when you come to a place like this, John. They put a guy out there who's insecure." He threw his hands up to gesture to the small, awkward, bleachers-on-one-side gymnasium with the cross behind the scorers' table. Jeff went in the locker room and changed out of his black Milan basketball golf shirt and khakis and put his tracksuit back on. As the game started, he hung out by the door of the locker room, peeking at the game. He wasn't sure whether or not he was allowed to sit in the stands to watch the game. Finally, as Milan struggled defensively in the first quarter and allowed nineteen points, he couldn't take it anymore and climbed into the bleachers.

At halftime, Milan was down 38–28 and looking every bit the team that Josh knew wasn't ready to play. Nothing was going right. When a play was actually run correctly, someone would miss a five-foot shot. Even though Trinity Lutheran had about a third of the students that Milan did, Trinity Lutheran was bigger and more physical. Every time Josh switched to zone to combat the size differences, a Milan player would forget his spot in the zone and give up an easy basket. Milan was also losing in fouls, with fifteen first-half fouls called on them against Trinity Lutheran's five. Zack Lewis held an icepack on a purple lump underneath his right eye. Milan's coaches thought it was worse than their boys not being ready to play; it was pretty clear to them that they were getting homered by the officials.

In the middle of the third quarter, with the game slipping away, Josh left his five starters on the bench to stare at the nineteen-point deficit on the scoreboard. It wasn't a punishment, necessarily, but there was no need to keep the starters in. They were frustrated. The normally quiet Kurtis Kimla had just about found himself in a fight at center court. A Trinity Lutheran player dove for the ball, practically tackling Kurtis in the process. As Kurtis stood up, with the Trinity Lutheran player still on his back, he pushed the boy with his arm and leg. Randy Combs looked down the bench at Josh and said, "Let's get through this last minute and four seconds without anything crazy happening."

On the bus ride home, the players knew better than to try and fool around like they did on the way there. The team's record was 2–2, the best start for Milan since the 2002–3 season, but Josh expected more. Even though he had known beating North Decatur would be a long shot, he had expected to beat Trinity Lutheran. Josh climbed the stairs of the bus, slumped in his seat, and pulled his black-and-gold sock cap low over his eyebrows. He opened his phone and started texting some of his coaching friends around the state to see how they did that night. Josh flipped through the Waldron folder, trying to prepare for the game the next night. Waldron would be a good matchup for Milan, and it would be at home. But Josh worried about how fresh the boys would be the night after a long, physical game. As the team left the bus, Josh said nothing except what time walkthrough would be in the morning. He was hoping to instill some sort of focus in them.

That night, as the boys walked to their cars in the frozen-over Milan High School parking lot, a snowball fight broke out. The boys threw snowballs at each other, using the younger players' moms' cars and vans as bunkers. Then it became more fun to throw the snowballs at those moms' cars and vans. White air left the boys' mouths, and though the cold showed evidence of deep breaths, the breathing was more relaxed than earlier in that gym in Seymour.

Inside, Josh sat slumped in his chair. There'd be two hours at least of film breakdown and preparation for Waldron the next night. His wife was probably just getting home from her shift at the hospital. They were trying—without much luck—to have a child, and the late nights were not helping the cause. Two and two was the best record they'd seen around here in a long time, but it wasn't the dominance the town hungered for, wasn't that 1954 team with Plump and Craft and White. Two and two didn't build museums, didn't hang banners, didn't make legends. Two and two wouldn't make Josh's job safe. The way the administration talked, and the way the governor cut education funding, nothing might. Back in his office, Josh opened a bag of Chex Mix he had bought earlier that day at the Jay-C. "Let's break it down," he said to Jeff and Tyler. And they did, late into the night.

If a 2–2 record caused Josh to stuff cotton balls in his ears to cut down on the stress, then 2–3 called for something stronger. Saturday night against Waldron was a slim loss but a loss that shouldn't have happened, in Josh's mind. Zack Lewis, perhaps still fired up over what happened at Trinity Lutheran, was in foul trouble all night and only played nine of the thirty-two minutes.

Milan players were used to limited chances. The Monday after the double-loss weekend to Trinity Lutheran and Waldron, the team was invited to practice at Conseco Fieldhouse, home of the Indiana Pacers in Indianapolis. After the practice, they stayed and watched the Pacers play the New Orleans Hornets. Josh knew he'd have to pitch in for a couple of the players to make the trip, and he always had a little bit of money set aside in his budget for things like that. When the trip was brought up back in October, Josh told the coaches that he liked the idea because it would get the kids to a big city; it would be a real nice chance to "get the boys out in the world."

When Milan players got chances, Josh expected them to capitalize on those chances. But, the day after visiting Indianapolis, the team struggled against tiny Hauser High School and lost by 13 points. It's not that the team didn't have an opportunity to win, but they consistently underperformed in clutch situations—especially when shooting free throws at key moments in the game. The team's declining free throw percentage was part of what Josh privately called the losing mentality of Milan. "Same ol' Milan," he'd say in a singsong, mocking tone, working on a scouting report on his computer. "We're not very big. We don't expect to win." Josh expected to win, and it was starting to rub off on the kids a little—two early wins were evidence of that. But free throws? Free throws were what Milan was supposed to be good at—the basics, stuff the players could practice on their own. Jimmy Chitwood shot free throws on the dirt court next to his barn, making every one while talking to Norman Dale. Free throws were a discipline, a routine. While each player had his own routine—some dribbling twice in front and once to the side, some not letting the ball touch the floor at all—they were expected to at least *have* a routine. Plus, this was southern Indiana. Not far down the road was Indiana University, where Bobby Knight used to tell his teams that he wanted them to make more free throws than the other team shot. The home of Steve Alford, from New Castle—the home of the biggest high school gymnasium in the world—whose free throw routine at Indiana was echoed by the student section: *Socks! Shorts!*

One, two, three . . . swish! That was the mid-eighties, and while the University of Houston's Phi Slamma Jamma was fresh in the minds of basketball fans, the crowds in that basketball-crazy state in flyover territory were chanting for free throw excellence.

Free throw woes were on Josh's mind. He had his team shoot free throws every day at practice. Instead of water breaks, they split up into pairs or threesomes on the six practice goals in the gym and shot five each, reporting their scores to Mary-Kate or Vicky. Josh wanted them shooting free throws tired, because that's how they'd shoot them in a game. At practice, when the pressure was off, the team was quite good, most boys hitting four of five or five of five. Games were something else entirely.

Josh was trying to get his boys to be more physical in practice, in order to get to the line more often. He knew they would likely settle down in game situations and make free throws, but as the Hauser game suggested, they were in danger of not being in that situation at all. With a team the size of Milan, Josh had hoped to play a more modern version of the 1954 team's style: get up by a few points by halftime and stall out the clock.

The plan seemed genius in its simplicity: make layups, make free throws. This wasn't a strategy based off a complicated offense, wasn't a strategy focused on difficult shots. The layups were there, all over the court. The problem was, the layups weren't going down. Against Hauser, the normally reliable John Herzog was only two of sixteen from the field. He was trying hard to seek contact, relying on the contact to get to the line rather than focusing on going up strong and trying to make a layup. Josh, in the practices right before and after Christmas, borrowed blocking pads from the football team. He had the boys go up for layups, and each time Josh would hit them in the side with the blocking pad, simulating body contact. At this point in the season, Josh had hoped to perfect a defensive press, maybe throw some new offensive sets into the mix. But with a 2–4 record and the conference season and county tournament looming, he was focusing on layups and free throws. Layups and free throws: the free points available to a team in basketball. The chances everyone on the court was permitted. For a team that didn't get many chances, they couldn't afford to waste the free ones.

6

ALL QUIET

Christmas Break: 2–4

The gym was quieter than normal. Milan had just tipped off against Southwestern in the South Dearborn Holiday Tournament at Hanover College, right on the Ohio River between Louisville, Kentucky, and Cincinnati. It was winter break, and no fans other than parents made the hour-long drive to Hanover to cheer on the team. Despite the 10 a.m. start, it was December 30 and far enough away from families' holiday celebrations for students and people in town to have a conflict. The team hoped that if they won the 10 a.m. game maybe word would spread and people would show up for the championship game of the tournament that evening.

The gym sounded like a frozen-over field in late December. Each squeak of the players' shoes reverberated off the walls the way the hawk's call does off a stand of trees near a field. Winter in Indiana has a sound, and the sound is mostly an echo, then a drifting into silence. Usually the sound is reserved for the outdoors, where few people explore during December, January, and February except for a run to the store or to gather with friends and family. Indiana's not as cold for as long as the northern states, so people grit their teeth for a couple of months and get through the winter by the fire or the heating ducts. Due to the absence of people and noise outside, and the crisp, icy air, you feel like you can hear things miles away. The Hanover College gym on December 30 sounded like this too—no cheerleaders or student sections (unless you counted the "student section" made up of the Scottsburg and South Decatur teams, watching the game before theirs). The squeaks of the players' shoes sounded like an army of field mice bouncing off a barn some distance away. When the referees called fouls, everyone in the gym could hear them tell the scorer who the foul was on, and for what. When players took foul shots, the gym was as still as a week-old snowdrift.

The beginning of the game was quiet as well. But halfway through the first quarter Josh broke the silence when Kurtis, after stealing a pass on the perimeter, dribbled down the court and decided to double pump on a mostly uncontested layup. He was expecting contact, he received none, and he missed the layup. Josh high-stepped from his perch on the scorers' bench and went down to Braden Voss to tell him to get in for Kurtis. Kurtis knew as soon as he missed the layup and the rebounding Southwestern player traveled that he was coming out of the game for the error. Without looking at Josh or waiting for the substitution horn to sound, Kurtis jogged off the court. After Josh sat Kurtis down in the first seat on the bench and yelled at him to play through contact, not play for contact, he put Kurtis right back in for Ethan Voss. Braden was becoming the only player off the bench Josh could trust, and even then he couldn't afford to have both Ethan and Braden in the game at the same time because they were weak defensively. They were the best shooters on the team, but their lack of strength and lateral quickness ensured that they would give up as many points as they scored or more.

They were a six-, maybe seven-player team. He couldn't afford to play guys like Nick Walter and Jake White and Alex Layden for more than eight to twelve minutes a game because they offered very little offensively. Jake—even though he was always the one texting Josh at night, asking him to come to school early and let him into the gym to shoot before school—was struggling with the best part of his game, shooting three-pointers. His flat shot attacked the rim like a fastball rather than a pop fly. His buildup and release were slow, and defenders could easily alter his shot. Worse yet, especially for a shooter, his confidence was dipping. Josh was considering having him play a little JV to help him find some confidence against easier, younger competition. Jake would have to find some offense somewhere, because, unlike Alex and Nick, Jake was not a very good defender. He was a slow six-foot guard on a team of average-speed six-foot guards.

One player whose feelings were not going to be hurt by Josh sticking with a six- or seven-player rotation was Derek Hornberger. The Hanover gym was made quieter by one less player on the Milan bench, one less set of parents in the crowd. Derek had wanted to quit before the South Decatur game back on December 10, but his parents—and the prospect of seeing Mary-Kate Jackson every day—had convinced him to try to stick it out. In 1954, fifty-eight boys tried out. In 2010, there were no cuts, and now a boy who was quitting.

Milan went into the half up 34–21 on Southwestern. The boys were excited to be winning by such a large margin at half, especially after losing three games in a row. The win seemed like it would be impressive, but Southwestern was going through some troubles of its own. For some reason, standout guard Jordan Yarbrough wasn't playing, and Josh had only a vague idea that he had been suspended for something. Southwestern wasn't very deep on the bench. For instance, senior Steve Adams wore wire-rim glasses, confident he wouldn't be played. B.J. McAllister, who last year was Southwestern's coach and had moved to coach his alma mater, Switzerland County, told Josh in the stands after the game that Steve had been stabbed in the arm a year or so prior. Why Steve was on the basketball team was a mystery—at nearly 275 pounds he looked like a dad rather than an athlete. B.J. was not at the South Dearborn Holiday Tournament to scout Steve Adams.

While the boys celebrated their first halftime lead since the South Decatur game three weeks earlier, Josh stood outside the locker room talking to Tyler Theising, Jeff Stutler, and Brad Voss (Braden, Ethan, and Alex's uncle), who kept unofficial stats on a PalmPilot for most of the games. Brad was the youngest of his generation of Voss boys and wore a cochlear implant on one of his ears. He was shorter than the other Vosses at about five-ten and was stocky. He sat a couple of rows behind the bench most games and would occasionally yell things to Josh like "Three fouls on Zack!" or "They're going zone again!" At halftime, he would stand and hike up the legs on his khaki pants—Brad always seemed to be wearing khakis—and stomp down the three or so bleacher seats to the floor, following Josh and the coaches off the court. Usually, due to Milan's deficit or poor refereeing or disappointing stats, Brad would have his head down and his mouth pursed and cocked to one side of his face, seemingly put there by a shake of his head. Brad arrived at the coaches' huddle outside the locker room during the Southwestern game with the usual clumsy gait.

"Three of fucking thirteen," Brad said, the words bouncing off the cement walls and floor outside Hanover College's training room. Coaches and players from all four teams were in the same corner of the Hanover athletic center, and

Josh, Tyler, and Jeff looked up at Brad both in agreement and with a look that said, "Let's not tell the whole world about our problems, eh?"

The celebratory mood in the locker room changed immediately when Josh walked in. Halftime of the two previous games hadn't been pretty, and neither were the postgame talks. Josh usually saved the more severe histrionics for his own office, but during halftime the previous week he kicked a trash can on his way into the locker room. People had started telling different stories about what Josh said next. A group of parents told John Prifogle that their boys said Josh pointed to the trash and said, "That's what you are. Trash." Josh told John that he did indeed kick the trash can and pointed to it, but what he said was, "That's what you're playing like. Trash." Either way, some parents were growing upset with Josh.

It wasn't too hard to see which parents were angry with Josh and which parents hoped he'd stick around. The angry ones—Nick Walter's parents, Kurtis Kimla's parents, and the parents of Russell Pitts (a clumsy sophomore center on the JV team) and Joey Davis (the JV point guard, a sophomore with good ball-handling skills but hampered by poor shooting and decision making)—started sitting closer together. With every game, they migrated from the top of the bleachers—where some of them sat for the South Decatur game at the beginning of the season—toward the bench. Against Southwestern, they were mid-height in the seats of Hanover College's gym, which featured comfortable NBA arena / movie theater–style seating behind the benches. Usually this group of parents would be sitting closer to one another, and they looked uncomfortable in the plush chairs separated by armrests.

They all had their own problems with Josh. The Walters, whose older son, Alex, had been a senior on Josh's first Milan team the year before, thought Josh was too much of a yeller. They thought that his outbursts—both in practice and at games—set a bad example for the boys. Josh, in their eyes, took basketball too seriously. They were also upset about a moment during last year's season when Josh took Alex out of a game and said, "Goddamn it, Alex," thinking he might have said, "Goddamn you, Alex."

Joey Davis's mom had concerns about Josh's language too—when she called John Prifogle, she complained about Josh's use of "Jesus Christ" around the boys. Joey's dad was mostly unhappy that his son was still on the junior varsity team. He took Joey's basketball career very seriously, instilling in him the importance of ball handling. And it was true: Milan lacked a true point guard—someone who could handle the ball and pass well. Zack Lewis was good enough but wasn't the type of flashy passer Joey's dad thought the team needed. As the season wore on and Joey's turnovers and foul count rose in the JV games, Joey's dad began to sit next to John Herzog's dad, with whom he would criticize Josh's game management skills. The Kimlas also sat nearby and seemed to be growing tired of Josh yelling at Kurtis every time he made a mistake, which was a growing problem this year for Kurtis. Last year he had been the team's best player. But as a junior, he couldn't get it going—missing assignments on defense, not being aggressive on the drive, and sometimes dribbling off his foot.

Luckily, the old guard in Milan remained in Josh's corner. After all, the two wins thus far in Josh's second year and the three wins last year were the same number of wins the team managed in the previous two full seasons before Josh arrived. The Vosses loved having Josh in Milan. Ethan and Braden Voss and Alex Layden often came down to Josh's office just to chat and respected what Josh was trying to do—change the losing mentality of the team. Brian Voss (Ethan and Braden's dad) often sent Josh e-mails about things he might try in games or a team he went to scout—not being pushy but just trying to be helpful. Brian's little brother Brad helped out with stats, and Alex's mom, Anne Marie, often had a plate of cookies for Josh before games. Josh and Jill were often welcome at the Laydens' house when the Lewises and the Vosses came over. Josh and Jill were becoming part of Milan's most prominent family.

Still, Josh was an outsider. And when the outsider comes to the small town and tries to change things in a loud way, really pushes the boys in practices and games, expects them to come to open gym during the summer and before school in the fall, it's hard for everyone to be on board. In some ways, it might have been harder for some fans to watch the team win a game or two each season by a close margin, lose to better teams by five or six, and stay in games until the final horn. The Milan players looked better than they used to, and while much of that was thanks to Josh's insistence that the boys hit the gym as much as possible, some of the dissenters were willing to write it off as native talent for this crop of players. A winning program was now in sight for Milan for the first time in years. This was a team that could make some noise in a tournament setting, where anything could—and once did—happen. And when that kind of thing seems possible, everyone has an opinion about how it should finally be accomplished. Whenever a play or a defense doesn't work when a team is on the brink, fans groan and are certain that a different play or defense would have been the cure. And that leads people to criticize the coach, especially when he's only twenty-eight years old and from a place like Anderson, a powerhouse basketball program in a midsize industrial city in central Indiana. Josh had a bit of swagger to him, and to those in the town predisposed to dislike him anyway, it could be interpreted as big-city cockiness, an air of arrogance.

No matter what the parents thought of him, it was clear Josh still had the attention and respect of his players. So when Josh walked into the Hanover College locker room, the small celebration of the halftime lead ended immediately. Instinctively, the players hung their heads. Josh had been mad in the hallway about the field goal percentage. Really mad. He could tolerate missed shots and botched plays, but he couldn't tolerate the source of the poor field goal percentage. This team was soft. They avoided contact at the rim instead of forcing themselves on the defense. They were, to put it in terms coaches love to use, the nail instead of the hammer. Despite how sloppy that initial Lawrenceburg win had been, it was the kind of behavior he wanted to see from his team: ferocious defense, hustle, aggressive play. Mistakes caused by trying too hard were preferred over mistakes caused by players trying to react to what the other team was doing.

Even though Josh was mad, he saw the players hang their heads the second he walked in. Maybe the complaints of the parents following the Hauser and Waldron games had gotten to him. Maybe he decided he needed to lighten up. Whatever it was, Josh suddenly struck a different, positive tone in the locker room. "I'm not mad," he started. It was a lie, but delivered well. It was believable. "Remember in practice when I was hitting you with the pads when you went up for a layup? I can't get out there with the pad during the games." Josh smiled. The boys were prepared for an ass-chewing about the three of thirteen effort from the field, but once a few of them caught on to the absurdity of what Josh said, they smiled too. "It's illegal for me to do that," Josh said, extending the joke. A few boys even chuckled at that one.

The good news, Josh told them, was that they couldn't get much worse at shooting layups, and they were up by thirteen points. Southwestern wasn't playing their preferred full-court press very much—the college-sized court was ten feet longer and gave Milan more space to break the press when it was on. It would also give Milan more space to run the stall offense.

It's hard to tell whether Josh's attitude in the locker room made any difference, but Milan cruised to the win in the second half. Their field goal percentage improved a bit, partially thanks to the wide-open looks the team discovered through their patient, stalling offense. Milan scored less in the second half—just nine points in each of the final two quarters—but that was the idea: long possessions on offense to take up time.

At this point in the season, a win was a win. Beating Southwestern meant busting a three-game losing streak. A lot of people had seen the Hauser loss coming. Even though Milan was playing its best basketball in years, Hauser started three players taller than Nick Ryan. Sometimes teams can overcome that kind of size difference, but it's usually via a dynamic scorer. Milan hadn't found that player yet—Josh thought Kurtis or Ethan or John could be that guy, but none of them had taken a game over yet. In the locker room after the game, Josh was quick to praise the team—well, the starters anyway, since they were still in the game with a minute left, with Milan up sixteen points—but made his praise short.

Ever since Josh had arrived in Milan, he talked privately—to his coaches, to his peers at other schools, to mentors, to friendly parents—about changing the mentality in Milan. He felt that because of recent history or local economics or the social depression evident in the town, Milan had a losing mentality. He couldn't pinpoint the source, but he knew the mentality ran deep. And it wasn't just a losing mentality about basketball. Restaurants, like the barbecue place in the BP station on the edge of town, opened while they were still renovating the inside because they were paying rent and needed cash flow right then. People around town spoke about the Milan football team with a disbelieving smile, as if to say *Wasn't that a magical run we were on?* Even when things were going well for something in town—the football team most recently—folks couldn't quite believe their luck. Wins in Milan were something you found on the ground in the parking lot, next to a heads-up penny. Young men in Milan expected to lose, expected to go to the local community college when they hoped to go to Indiana or Purdue University, expected to go bankrupt if they started a business, expected their friends and family to die early. *Hoosiers* never felt so far away in the year 2010 because the movie felt like a bigger and bigger fictionalization. Jimmy Chitwood promising coach he'd make it? In 2010 it seemed harder and harder to even get a shot off.

For that reason exactly, Josh wanted the celebration to end but for the momentum and mentality created by the win to continue. "Tonight, we play for a championship, boys," Josh said, rubbing the palms of his hands together in anticipation. "The first of many we'll play for this season. Playing in championship games puts us one step closer to where we want to be as a program."

Josh collected the boys in the middle of the locker room, the same poured concrete floor below him that had been in the Milan locker room for less positive talks after the Waldron and Hauser games.

"The road to a championship in March starts tonight, men." In an instant, Josh had stopped referring to the team as boys and decided on men. He hoped they would grow up that fast. So much relied on those teenagers in black and gold. While the South Dearborn Holiday Tournament might not bring back the heyday of 1950s Milan, might not jump-start the town's economy, it would be a start. If this team could get its mind right, could believe in itself, what would stop Milan as a whole from doing the same? Even though the win-loss record didn't look anything like the 1953 and 1954 teams', one thing in Milan was still true. Basketball mattered.

"State on three," Josh started. The young men in the huddle looked each other in the eye rather than stare at the pile of hands in the middle of their circle. This is why basketball mattered: there were eleven boys and three coaches and one stat keeper who all believed that a collection of people from Milan, Indiana, could do something great. In unison, those fifteen shouted the words that, if they were improbable in 1954, were nearly impossible in 2010: "One, two, three, State!"

7

THE EXPENDABLES

First Championship Game: 3–4

After beating Southwestern, everyone piled into the minibus and headed to Mr. Gatti's Pizza in Madison, a sad combination of Cici's Pizza buffet and Chuck E. Cheese ten minutes from Hanover College. For many teams at an all-day tournament, the school's budget would have allowed for a team meal in between games, somewhere the players could get a lunch of good carbohydrates and proteins, someplace even with a small room in the back where the team could go over strategy for the next game.

There would be no team meetings or healthy lunches at Mr. Gatti's. Josh ordered his buffet last, making sure all the players had enough money to cover their lunch. Even the players like Ethan Voss and Alex Layden who knew not to load themselves down with the equivalent of an entire large pizza, who knew enough to get a bowl of salad and drink something noncarbonated, opted for ranch dressing and bacon bits and snuck in a couple of glasses of Mountain Dew or Dr. Pepper. The team broke up in the small dining room and sat three to a table. The room was mostly silent—the only noises were guttural sounds of approval when the big-screen television in the dining room showed college basketball highlights. The boys in the room came from a decent collection of fandoms and rooted for regional schools in varying degrees of rivalry. Logan Alloway was a Louisville fan, Ethan Voss rooted for Purdue—he was hoping to be the team's manager when he went to school there next year—and there were fans of Kentucky and Indiana.

Josh, an Indiana fan, now claimed Butler as his secondary team, as most people in the state had done. People around the state could be Butler fans *and* fans of their traditional teams because Butler wasn't a rival of Indiana, Purdue, Notre Dame, Louisville, Cincinnati, or Kentucky. Butler was just that small school in Indianapolis that played in the gym where Milan won its state championship in 1954, the same gym where Gene Hackman asks his players to measure the height of the rim, just to make sure Hinkle Fieldhouse was the same size as their court back in Hickory. Butler had captured the imagination of Hoosiers the state over because no one expected them to be playing Duke in a championship game in April 2010, and no one expected them to come so close to winning on a half-court Gordon Hayward heave.

The Butler team was composed of players who may have been recruited by Big Ten teams or Louisville or Cincinnati but were told that they would be role players or perhaps even walk-ons. They were a team made up of players like Matt Howard from tiny Crawfordsville, Indiana, who were too small to play their natural position, or like Shelvin Mack from Louisville, Kentucky, who wasn't considered a scoring threat at the Division I level. They were led by a young coach named Brad Stevens who left a corporate job in Indianapolis to follow his dream of being a college basketball coach.

Brad Stevens, even though he was a collegiate point guard at DePauw University, a Division III school in Greencastle, Indiana, looked more like Clark Kent than Superman. He didn't look like other coaches—Jay Wright at Villanova or Matt Painter at Purdue or Thad Matta, a former Butler coach himself, at Ohio State—big, imposing presences on the sideline, men who looked like they could still dunk with two hands, men who looked slick in pinstripe suits. Brad Stevens was short and skinny, and looked like the junior executive he once was, like he might have a business card and a graphing calculator in his jacket's breast pocket. Butler was easy to root for because the team reminded Hoosiers of their high school teams—quirky, uniquely skilled, and in any given March good enough to win it all. Now, especially since the 1999 advent of multiclass high school basketball tournaments in Indiana, Butler reminded everyone that a small school could tangle with the big boys and win. That narrative—the one made famous by Milan in 1954—had run the risk of disappearing with class basketball. Butler was in the position to bring back Hoosier Hysteria for everyone.

But, against all odds, some players on the Milan team found Butler unwatchable. They didn't get up and down the court like Cincinnati or Louisville or Kentucky. Where were the alley-oops, the dunks, the circus passes? Butler bored their opponents into submission on offense, using the entire shot clock to isolate Matt Howard in the block or set Gordon Hayward or Shelvin Mack up for a clear three-pointer. Butler grinded on offense until they got an H-O-R-S-E shot. Everyone could hit an H-O-R-S-E shot—the boys had heard Josh tell them that every time they let someone get wide open while practicing defense. Butler spent all their energy on defense, playing a strict man-to-man until Matt Howard got in foul trouble (he always did). They played aggressive defense, they cut off the passing lanes, they played high on their man on the perimeter, knowing the frontcourt players would rotate over if the guards got beat off the dribble. It wasn't flashy. It wasn't games with both teams scoring 90 or 100. It was team basketball with very few highlights. It was the way Milan could play, the only possible way for Milan to play winning basketball. For the Kentucky and Louisville fans of Milan, it wasn't the stuff dreams were made of. But it was their best reality.

After about an hour and a half of lounging at Mr. Gatti's, Jeff loaded the team in the minibus and started driving toward B.J. McAlister's house in Hanover. B.J. was Josh's best friend in coaching. They had been assistants and JV coaches together at New Albany High School, a large school in southern Indiana and a basketball powerhouse. They met when they were in their early twenties, young and figuring out how to coach high school basketball. B.J. left for the Southwestern job in the 2008–9 school year, and Josh left for Milan the next year. B.J. thought it was the job of his lifetime, but when Switzerland County announced their head basketball coach position, he was first in line to apply for the job. Coaching his high school basketball team, even in tiny Vevay, Indiana, was B.J.'s dream job.

B.J. hadn't had any luck selling his small, new-construction vinyl-sided house near Hanover's campus. Since Vevay was about thirty miles and fifty minutes from Hanover—even though they looked close on a map, the number of winding state roads necessary to get from Hanover to Vevay made a nightly commute, especially for a high school basketball coach, inconceivable—B.J. had moved in with his parents in Vevay. It wasn't an ideal setup, especially for a single man in his late twenties, but until he could sell his house, B.J. had little other choice. So B.J.'s house—still set up with couches and furniture and a big-screen TV with surround sound—made it the perfect place for a basketball team to crash for a few hours before they played in a championship game.

At B.J.'s house, Josh popped *The Expendables* into the DVD player for the team and joined B.J. in the kitchen. He was quick to poke fun at Josh.

"Starters in, up 16, with a minute left, Coach?" B.J. asked, smiling.

"Hell, all we have is starters," Josh said, sitting at the high-top pub style table in the corner of the kitchen. "I can only trust about six or seven players right now."

"Ain't New Albany, is it?" B.J. smiled. At New Albany, Josh and B.J. didn't have to worry about enough talent; they had to worry about keeping skilled players interested in playing team basketball: learning plays, playing tough defense, not taking quick, low-percentage shots. Now, in the Ohio River Valley Conference—a collection of 1A and 2A schools along the Ohio River in southwestern Indiana—they were both more worried about getting a full team of kids who actually knew how to play basketball at a high level.

Life in a small-town basketball program had changed dramatically since the 1950s, more dramatically than *Hoosiers* reflected. The day of his first practice as coach, Gene Hackman's character, Norman Dale, walks into the small Hickory gym as George is putting the team through a scrimmage. The gym is dark except for light shining in from the waxy windows near the roof, above the last of the ten or so rows of bleachers on either side of the court. Jimmy Chitwood has not yet decided to join the team, leaving Hickory with just six players—well, five and a half, as the diminutive Ollie would tell you. As Norman Dale tells George that his coaching days are over, George responds by saying, "Look, mister, there's two kinds of dumb: a guy that gets naked and runs out in the snow and barks at the moon, and a guy who does the same thing in my living room. First one don't matter, the second one you're kinda forced to deal with." Norman looks at his team. *Six players,* he might be thinking, because he looks each one of them in the eye before he talks.

In *Hoosiers*, Norman Dale shrugs off his worries about such a thin team. After all, Hickory only has 161 students—both boys and girls. And that's where 1952 Hickory and 1954 Milan intersect—in 1954, Milan had 161 students as well. The difference? Of those 161, 73 were boys. And of those 73 boys, 58 tried out for the basketball team. There were no freshman teams or junior varsity teams. If all things were equal, a boy had less than a 20 percent chance of making the basketball team in tiny Milan, Indiana, in 1954. While *Hoosiers* seems to accurately capture the town's attitude regarding their boys and their sport—they couldn't get enough!—it is fiction in this way: if you were a boy between the ages of fourteen and eighteen in Milan, you most likely tried to join the basketball team. The "us-against-the-world"—or at least "us-against-the-town"—mentality Norman Dale instilled in his Huskers wasn't an option for Marvin Wood in real-life 1954 Milan. Basketball was played in alleys next to manure piles, debated in barbershops, watched in a packed gym on a Friday or Saturday night. High school basketball was Milan's movie theater, bowling alley, and dance hall all in one. Who wouldn't want to be the focus of the town for four years?

Josh was starting to understand that a basketball life in Milan in 2010 was a shaky one at best, especially when dealing with parents. And even B.J.—considered by most in the area to be a good young coach just like Josh—had his share of complaints as he tried to change things at Southwestern, which was often considered a lightweight program in the region. B.J. had managed a 16–28 record at Southwestern. For a young, inexperienced coach, it seemed impressive. Still, when the *Madison Courier* ran the article about B.J. leaving for Switzerland County, reaction was mixed on the newspaper's website. The first comment about B.J. leaving was: "The best thing that has EVER happened to SW schools! All he cared about was winning and really did not care for the kids. He won't be missed by too many. I would bet that there will be many more participants to play basketball next year."

It was hard to imagine that poster's allegations as truth. B.J. had spent his midtwenties in Hanover, Indiana, spending up to fourteen hours a day in the school building during basketball season. At the same time, the poster represented a group of people in town. B.J. was an outsider, and tough. If B.J. didn't bring the town at least a sectional championship, some people weren't going to like him no matter what he did. It was hard for Josh not to see some of himself in B.J.—even Jill knew that they were very similar coaches, since they both based their style on their mentor at New Albany, Jim Shannon—and it added a little doubt in Josh's mind about the parents in town who were growing restless with his aggressive style. Josh, too, was an outsider in Milan, and while he was improving upon Milan's past performance, his team wasn't setting the world on fire, either. Josh sat at the kitchen table and seemed to allow himself a moment to think, perhaps about his future and Milan. But only a minute. Josh collected the South Dearborn scouting report. There was a championship to win that evening.

In the living room, half of the team had fallen asleep to the mortar shells and gunfire of *The Expendables*. In the movie—essentially a buddy movie with several buddies, a team movie—the characters are mostly past their prime, just like the actors, but each time one is in trouble, the entire team bails him out.

Usually this occurs via a storm of heavy explosives. Terry Crews looks at Jet Li in a moment of duress. "Great, they got a small army. What have we got?" he asks. Crews considers Li for a moment and answers his own question. "Four and a half men." Still, the undersized crew pushes on and succeeds—the high-budget *Hoosiers.*

When the movie ended, Josh walked into B.J.'s living room and flipped on the lights. The boys knew well enough to respond right away rather than pull the same trick they pulled on their parents on Sunday mornings at home. Coach was ready. Time to wake up. Josh walked to the DVD player, took out *The Expendables*, and put in a South Dearborn game tape.

"This is the first of many championship games we'll play this year, guys," Josh said, stepping over the boys' legs as he passed out the South Dearborn scouting reports. His tone said, *So, get used to it.* It was just the South Dearborn Holiday Tournament, but it was a tournament with a championship game, and good teams won championship games, no matter what the level of the tournament. Ethan Voss sat on the couch—a senior's position—not on the floor like his little brother and the rest of the underclassmen, and stared intently at the scouting report. *This is a championship game,* he thought. Ethan had waited so long for a championship to come to Milan. He nudged his cousin Alex on the couch when Josh started talking big. They didn't need to talk about what could be, what tonight could be the start of. They had dreamed the same dream their whole lives, and now they had the opportunity to live it. Alex cracked a smile when Ethan nudged him. They had played this game and the games it could lead to in their bedrooms with Nerf hoops and in the kitchen with balls of used paper towels and in their driveways when the sun was barely visible through the rotting cornstalks left behind after harvest. They knew how their game ended. Bobby Plump hits the last shot.

In the first quarter against South Dearborn, it was clear that their dream was turning into a nightmare. After six minutes ran off the clock to start the game, Milan had six turnovers. Ethan was missing nearly everything, including an air-ball three-point shot from the corner, usually his specialty. With just over three minutes left in the first quarter, Ethan and John ran into each other on their cuts. All Josh could do was throw his hands up in the air after every silly mistake, a travel or a bad pass or a double dribble. "Basics!" he yelled. Earlier in the season, it had been free throws. Now it was simply keeping possession on offense long enough to get a shot up. Once again, the team that had far fewer chances given to them—in life, by their lack of size, by their lack of native ability—were wasting the few they had.

Finally, midway through the third quarter, after Ethan had missed two more three-point shots (he hadn't hit one all game and finished 0 for 7), Josh put his younger brother Braden in the game. Braden was a few inches shorter but also a tad quicker. Both had technically beautiful shooting strokes from long distance, and Josh often made this substitution. Having Braden and Ethan in the game at the same time would give them two great shooters, yes, but both Voss boys at one time would create a liability on defense. They were like-for-like substitutions, often, sharing the minutes of the game.

Braden made his minutes count in the third quarter. Lately he had become especially adept at faking a three-pointer and driving to the basket. Teams in southwestern Indiana knew each other, and until recently Braden had been like his brother—a catch-and-shoot player and little more. Ethan was six feet three, though, allowing him to get his shot off more frequently. Braden was listed as six one but was actually more like six feet even, meaning he had less height on his release point. Plus, if defenders were going to come flying in and the post defense wasn't going to rotate over to protect against him driving, why not take it to the basket? He was up for playing against tougher opponents, matching their strength with his speed and basketball acumen. This trait would serve Braden well as a Milan basketball player, it seemed. When was Milan the bigger, stronger team? Almost never.

It's often said that the mark of a good team or a good player is that you can tell the other team what you're going to do on offense and still, with that knowledge, they cannot stop you. Sports clichés are often based on this idea, with hammers and nails being the preferred metaphor. Legend has it that one time Larry Bird pointed to a spot on the floor and told Seattle SuperSonics forward Xavier McDaniel late in a game, "I'm going to get the ball right here and I am going to bury it in your face." McDaniel responded by saying, "I know. I'll be waiting." After cutting twice, planting on the exact spot where he'd pointed, and making the shot that put the Celtics ahead for good, Bird looked at McDaniel and said, "I didn't mean to leave two seconds on the clock."

So, at the end of the third quarter, when John Herzog stood at half-court for fifty seconds to try to pull South Dearborn out of their zone defense, and when South Dearborn refused to move to man-to-man to pressure John, messages were sent. Milan was saying, "John Herzog is going to drive to the basket and make it." South Dearborn was saying, "We know. We'll be waiting." When John

Herzog drove right past his defender, spun to the left, leaned into him, and made an eight-foot shot to put Milan up 37–36, it surprised everyone on the court. A Milan player had said—through actions (John was too quiet a kid to trash talk like Bird)—that he was going to do something. South Dearborn knew it, and it didn't matter. Milan had just imposed their will on another team in a championship game. Now, all they had to do was finish.

8

GAMES WITHIN THE GAME

First Championship Game: 3–4

If getting the Milan team comfortable with the idea of winning—from the current squad to the youth players he coached one day a week with the Milan Youth Basketball League to the "team" of the entire Milan community—was part of the larger job Josh envisioned himself tackling when he took the Milan coaching job a year and a half ago, then the talk he gave the team in between the third and fourth quarters of the South Dearborn game was a microcosm of the work he hoped to do at the small school in southwestern Indiana. Often, basketball coaches provide little games within the game to get players to think about the second-to-second decisions that occur on the court. Winning the first and last minute of every quarter is one of these minigames that coaches—including Josh—provide the players in order to keep them thinking small. A thirty-two-minute game can seem a large endeavor for a team, just as a twenty-one-game season (more for those lucky and skilled enough to make it past their first postseason game) can seem overwhelming to a school's fans. Coaches, and fans too, also look at two-, three-, and four-year records as a marker of their school's success. It can become distracting for individual players and each year's teams to think about such large-picture ideas.

Basketball, by nature, is a game of runs. Watch a basketball game on television, and the production crew will remind viewers of the runs each team goes on. Teams go without field goals for minutes at a time. Schools, like Milan, go without wins for games at a time. Teams who go on a losing streak—whether for minutes or games or years—suddenly think that they can't do anything right, that a teammate won't be in the correct spot on an offensive set or on defense because that's what they're used to in a losing run. Teams who get hot—again, for minutes or games—suddenly think that even if a player isn't in the right spot or a shot taken wasn't the shot envisioned by the coaching staff, it is still a good option because it puts two points on the scoreboard or a string of wins in the box score of a newspaper.

In between the third and fourth quarters, with Milan beating South Dearborn 37–36, Milan was in the middle of one of their best streaks. They had just won their morning game, ending a run of three losses. So when, after almost a minute of time had run off the clock, Braden Voss hit an open three-pointer from the wing, Josh pumped his fist and sat on the bench. It was the perfect start to the fourth quarter: the maximum number of points from the field, and a minute off the clock. Milan had won its first minigame of the fourth quarter by a score of 3–0. The game was no longer Milan versus South Dearborn. The game was now Milan versus South Dearborn, Milan versus the clock, Milan versus Milan. Back when David beat Goliath, when Milan beat anyone who dared to step on the court, Milan's players were the kings of the minigames. They ran an offense called cat-and-mouse, in which they would hold the ball for long periods of time. They took care of the little things, and the little things took care of them. David used to live here. Josh was trying to move that David kid back into the district.

South Dearborn felt the crunch of the minigames on the court too. On their next possession, one of the supporting players heaved a quick three-point attempt, hoping to match points with Milan. The shot missed, and Milan rebounded. Despite Josh's orders to slow down, Kurtis faked a drive and pulled up from inside the arc, missing. Since they had the lead, each possession meant so much to Milan—they wanted to score, but they wanted to score after they took time off the clock. These minigames and long possessions were designed to make the game smaller, to erase the imbalance of talent between Milan and South Dearborn, to give Milan an even playing field.

After three minutes had passed in the fourth quarter, Milan had held on to their four-point lead. A stalemate, at this point, was as valuable to them as a win.

With four minutes left, Milan seemed to forget they were playing with the lead. They simply weren't used to controlling the game in the fourth quarter. Instead of treasuring each possession, they reverted to their normal fourth-quarter play. Milan was used to pushing the ball up the court, looking for ways to get back into a game at the very end. Suddenly, South Dearborn was up four points with three minutes left. Milan lost the minigame in the middle of the fourth quarter, and Josh called a time-out to settle the team down, to keep them focused on the next possession rather than encourage the boys to keep up with the frantic pace the game had taken on.

The time-out gave South Dearborn time to regroup and focus as well, and Milan was met with tough defense on their next possession. The best shot they could muster came from John Herzog, who dribbled baseline, spun to the basket, and shot a fadeaway jumper that missed.

There were two minutes left in the game, but a Milan win was no longer in reach. The players on the Milan bench seemed to sigh in unison as a lanky South Dearborn player took a powerful step to the rim and did what no Milan player could do in a game situation: dunk. South Dearborn had all the momentum, all the athleticism, all the control. They had simply stuck around for twenty-eight minutes, then pounced for two. A team like South Dearborn could afford such a long stretch of mediocrity because they had such native talent and athleticism. Milan had proved all season that they could not—that they had to win every small game within the game to give themselves a chance to win the overall game in the end. Milan lost 52–42.

After the game, Josh scanned his locker room, looking for answers. Just when Josh felt like Milan was gaining momentum, when the win was all but secured, they couldn't finish. His eyes found two starters: Ethan Voss and Kurtis Kimla.

Josh couldn't figure Kurtis out. The year before, Kurtis had led the team in scoring and rebounding as a sophomore. Back in October at the first coaches' meeting, Josh and Jeff told Tyler all about how Kurtis would once again be the team's standout. Despite his dad's rough exterior—he wore a leather jacket and a bandana on his head, giving him a "biker-tough" look—Josh knew Kurtis was coddled at home. He walked around school and practice and the locker room with a closed-mouth half-smile and slumped shoulders. Josh often called Kurtis the best athlete in Milan, but he never looked the part, never looked aggressive or ready for action. He would get subbed out of a game and walk off the court without the appropriate expression—good or bad—and slump in his spot on the bench. It didn't seem like Kurtis was disinterested (although sometimes Josh accused him of that), just that he was a passive person. Milan needed Kurtis to change.

Like Kurtis, Ethan was struggling as well, with only nine for thirty-four in the season from behind the three-point line after the South Dearborn tournament. The only player on the Milan team to truly buy into the history, it wasn't how he expected his senior season to go. Ethan's minutes were slipping because his little brother Braden was successful coming off the bench. Even though Ethan started, Braden had played six more minutes on the season and was shooting a bit better from long distance at 33 percent.

Ethan and Kurtis were responding to their changing roles in different ways. Ethan continued to be a quiet yet positive presence, sharing notes with Braden about how to get open on certain plays during breaks in practice or film sessions. Ethan had rare awareness for an eighteen-year-old. His grandfather and great-uncles and uncles played for Milan. He'd been honing his jump shot from an early age on the driveway with his family, and he and Braden had talked about winning together at Milan since they were in elementary school. They didn't talk about sharing minutes or the struggles they might face. They talked about restoring glory, the big picture for their team and town, not what to do when the team went minutes without a bucket or what to do when they couldn't get a stop on defense. Dreams aren't made of grinding through possessions; dreams are made of last-second shots to win a county tournament or sectional championship. No matter the specific dreams Ethan had, the overall dream was being a part of a winning team in Milan, and Ethan was ready to accept any role that made that happen with grace. Basketball was a big part of Ethan's identity. He was proud to be a part of a historic program, and hoped to be the manager of the men's basketball team when he attended Purdue the next fall.

The Purdue dream, however, was a dream for another day. On January 5, as Ethan sat in the back of the bus headed to South Ripley for the first game of the county tournament, he rested his head against the window while the other boys listened to their iPods or read the text messages that collected on their phones as the bus hit the invisible line south of Milan where cell phone service kicked in. Ethan was a normal teenager in some ways—interested in girls, interested in his friends' comings and goings—but he brought a precocious mental preparation to game days. The bus ride was reserved for one last look at the scouting report and running plays over and over in his mind. He worked through game scenarios in his mind—where to cut on certain plays if the defense forced him a certain way, who might be open if his shot wasn't available.

As the bus passed through the bleak gray late afternoon, past the sparse, muddy cornfields on State Road 101, he imagined coming off of a baseline cut and catching the ball. As he closed his eyes, he searched for the sweet spot on the ball, put the pad of his right middle finger on the valve. Catch, flip the wrist, release. Three points. He had played South Ripley many times before, knew who would be guarding him, knew where the holes in South Ripley's zone might be. They would play a zone, wouldn't they? They'd expect Ethan to continue to struggle shooting the ball. *Come off the screen a little higher,* Ethan thought. *Find the gap in the zone. Force South Ripley to guard me, and John can get his points.*

It had been seven years since Milan won a game in the four-team Ripley County Tournament. Ethan was only eleven years old when Milan beat Jac-Cen-Del in the consolation game of the 2003–4 county tournament. No matter. *Catch. Flip. Release.*

It had been longer still since Milan had managed to win the entire thing. In 1999 and 2000, Milan made it to the championship game and lost, ending a first-round losing streak dating back to 1965 when Milan lost to the now-closed Versailles High School in the final by thirty-five points. Milan had slipped a long way from the dominant fifties, when they made the championship game all but one year and won six Ripley County titles. Five in a row from 1952 to 1956. *Catch. Flip. Release.* Ethan looked down at his scouting report, the one that had "RETURN TO GLORY" printed in capital letters at the top. The return had to start somewhere, and Ethan thought the short bus ride to South Ripley was as good a place and time as any to begin.

The game started, and Ethan was looking lost. As Milan went into halftime tied with South Ripley at 16–16, the game looked like something that would be played in a YMCA on a Saturday morning—bricked shots of all kinds, pileups for loose balls, missed layups.

It wasn't the ugliness that had Josh concerned; it was the lack of attention to little things. Josh wasn't going to go into the locker room and tell a group of boys to start making their shots. What would be the point in that? *Try harder to make the ball go through the hoop* would just produce more overthought, overaimed, over-the-rim shots. Before he entered the locker room, Josh was still mad about a certain play in the second quarter. Ethan had failed to pick up South Ripley's Jerad Walters on a fast break, instead deciding to stay closer to his man. Walters was clearly the most dangerous player on the break for

South Ripley, and Ethan should have moved over to contest the shot. As Brad Voss walked up to Josh, Jeff, and Tyler, apologizing for getting off work late and missing many of the first-quarter stats, Jeff said, "How do you not pick up Walters in transition?" Josh thought about his words carefully, took a moment. He crouched against the wall, as he often did at halftime when he was frustrated, the look of someone who was about to throw up and faint but unsure of the order of those two things. "Because Ethan Voss is a vagina?" Josh asked.

While Josh's words were shocking, so was the lack of compassion he held for Ethan. They were kindred spirits, Ethan and Josh, if only Josh took the time to realize it. Josh came to Milan because it was an open job, but he was excited to come because there was a chance to turn around the most famous basketball program in the state. Josh was a true believer, just like Ethan.

Josh knew he couldn't bring that kind of attitude into the locker room. That's what his little conferences at halftime with the coaches seemed to be about: adults letting off steam and every now and then poking fun at one of the players' actions on the court. That way, the halftime message could be focused and instructive. Josh walked into the locker room smiling and shaking his head.

"You know, Braden," Josh started, looking out of the corner of his eye to see Braden leaning back against a locker with a towel over his head, embarrassed by his shooting, "one time in high school we were playing at Richmond. The Tiernon Center. Big freaking gym. I shot a three off the side of the backboard." Josh looked at Braden. "I'm still alive. Keep shooting."

"Now, boys, the shots will fall. We're too good of a shooting team not to think that. But the thing I can't understand is: some people still don't know what to do on offense."

Ethan looked up. He had cut the wrong way on a play in the second half and put the whole possession off-kilter. He nodded.

"Freaking act like it, son!" Josh stalked around the locker room. "We are somehow in this game. And, you know, it's not all that different from a March atmosphere. Heck, we'll probably get this same locker room for sectionals, 'cause sectionals is here this year."

Ethan perked up at the word "March." It struck him in that moment that not only was the championship season right around the corner, it would be his last. Instead of looking down and swallowing hard, the usually timid Ethan met Josh's eyes.

"What wins sectional games, boys?" Josh asked, assuming no one would respond.

"The little things," Ethan replied. "Knowing where to go on a play. Blocking out for a rebound. Getting to the floor for loose balls."

Milan's first points of the third quarter were scored by Ethan on a three. Earlier that day, as he sat in the back of the bus thinking of all big shots he'd make, he didn't picture one—his first made shot—coming after being chewed out at halftime. He was rarely yelled at because he rarely made mistakes. He wasn't the quickest player (in fact, he might have been the slowest on the Milan team), but he usually put himself in good positions to make up for his lack of athleticism. *Catch. Flip. Release.*

Thanks to Ethan's motivating start, Milan won the third quarter. The team was patient for once, even if it wasn't productive patience at times. They worked the ball around the perimeter, making the zone slide to the left and to the right, trying to find the right time to attack. Even Kurtis was doing some of the attacking, knifing in from the wing and either pulling up for a jump shot or going all the way for a layup. With just eight minutes to play, Milan was up 31–29, nearly doubling their point production in the previous two quarters.

Then things went dry. It wasn't that Milan didn't have plenty of chances. South Ripley was making good shots like they had all third quarter—like Milan had, too. Milan had the added benefit of entering the fourth quarter one South Ripley foul away from the bonus. At that point, each little South Ripley push or hand-check meant Milan would shoot free throws. Milan had only three team fouls, which was also to their advantage.

But Milan missed five of twelve free throws. After every miss, Josh would stomp his foot and either slap both of his hands on the outside of his legs or put his hands on his head. He would gesture to the Milan parents behind the bench with his arms out as if to say, *I can lead the horse to water but I can't make him hit free throws.* Adding to the frustration were the seven turnovers of all sorts—double dribbles, travels, passes through a teammate's legs—that Milan committed in the fourth quarter. Seven possessions, wasted. Milan was in control until the weight of those closing minutes seemed to paralyze the boys.

The team walked out of the gym, down the hallway past the concession stand, past the South Ripley locker room, and past the girls' locker room the Jac-Cen-Del team was using. As Jac-Cen-Del jogged out to warm up for their game against Batesville, Josh turned to Jeff. "Tell me something, Jeff. Am I missing something? I mean, South Ripley isn't that good, are they?" Jeff shook his head no. "Why can't we close a game out?" Jeff treated it as a rhetorical question, or maybe Jeff just didn't have an answer.

When Milan finally got to their locker room, in the auxiliary gym, Josh didn't take his normal postgame stance of bending over at a ninety-degree angle, hands on knees. He stood up and leaned his head back against the wall, as if he were asking God to take him somewhere, anywhere, other than there. He didn't care that he looked like a man totally drained and defeated as the Batesville coaching staff and players walked past toward the court.

"Jesus, it's like they clone them up there," Josh said as the Batesville team walked by. They did look cloned, and their roster showed it: one player under six feet, most players between six three and six five. The Batesville team was muscular—they had shoulders where Milan had shirtsleeves. They were mostly brown-haired, mostly angular-faced, mostly thick-browed, mostly angry-looking. Batesville was the big school in Ripley County, the team that could skate through the Ripley County Tournament without much effort. They had conference championships and sectional championships to think about, unlike Milan and South Ripley and Jac-Cen-Del, for whom a Ripley County Tournament title would be a coup. Batesville was a team of winners.

Josh was acutely aware that Milan was not. They had battled all game to lose their grip in the closing minutes yet again. They had missed free throws; they had turned the ball over in new and inventive ways; they had done nothing to capitalize on the chances every basketball team is afforded in every game. They limited themselves.

"Losing mentality," Josh said, rubbing his eyes. He readjusted the cotton in his ears, which were red and must have been throbbing from the stress. "Same old Milan."

9

CHANGE FOR THE NICE BOYS

County Tournament: 3–6

Randy Combs walked into the coaches' office and saw Josh sitting at Randy's old desk, checking area scores on his old computer. Randy had a dress shirt and his Milan golf shirt on hangers in his hand. Randy looked at Josh's dress shirt and tie hanging on the handle to the file cabinet in between his desk and the football coach's desk. "Wearin' a tie?" Randy said, looking for Josh's golf shirt. It wasn't to be found. "You're shittin' me."

Randy sat down at the football desk and picked up the phone. He dialed Jeff Stutler's number from memory. "Jeff. We're wearing a tie." Randy paused. "I know, that's what I said."

It was a consolation game, after all. Josh shook his head not so much at Randy—because Josh hadn't yet looked up at him—but because of him. Randy enjoyed his role of consultant and eighth-grade coach for Milan after a full career of head coaching responsibilities at the school before he said enough was enough and he wanted to spend more time with his daughter, who was entering high school. That's when Milan hired Josh, and from the start Josh wanted Randy around. Milan was Josh's first head coaching job, and he earned the job when he was only twenty-seven. While Josh had been interested in coaching from a young age—he commuted from Ball State in Muncie to Anderson to coach his alma mater's freshman team when he was in college—he still had a lot to learn about coaching, and he knew it.

Perhaps the biggest thing Josh had to learn from Randy, though, was how to be Milan's coach. Not just *a* coach, *Milan's* coach. It had taken Randy a long time not to feel like an outsider in Milan—despite having a family that he moved to town—and Josh felt similarly. It was hard to come to a place like Milan as a coach with no ties to the town. For one, it was difficult to understand how to reach out to the community. Milan as a town exists in about a square half-mile next to the blinking-stoplight intersection of State Roads 101 and 350. There is a Dairy Queen, a low-cost grocery store named the Jay-C, a Family Dollar, a diner named the Reservation, three used car lots, a bank or two, the school, a small library, just under a dozen churches, and some run-down Victorian houses that are mostly rentals. Roselyn McKittrick operates the Milan '54 Museum and an antique store. Most people in Milan actually live just outside Milan, and many don't even shop, eat out, or go inside the town limits unless it's to pick a kid up at school or go to a basketball or football game. There's no real way to gain any political capital as an outsider in Milan by just being around town, because no one is ever around town. Plus, Josh was living on Lake Santee, even though it was an odd sort of living during basketball season, since he often put in twelve to fourteen hours a day at school.

The Milan coach had the added pressure and work of communicating with the members of the 1954 state championship team. The '54 team was a great fund-raising resource for the current program—they held a golf tournament and reunion every summer to raise money for jerseys and equipment—but it was a part of the job that most high school basketball coaches didn't have. Plus, to spend time planning events for state champions when the current team was struggling to win three games a year was more than an obvious irony—it could be downright embarrassing. Randy had succeeded in his time as Milan's coach, won a few sectional games, produced his share of winning records. He knew how to navigate Milan as an outsider to the extent that many didn't think of him as an outsider anymore. Josh knew he needed to emulate Randy.

Randy wasn't in the coaches' office that Saturday to help Josh understand local politics, though. He was there to help Josh diagnose exactly what was wrong with the team. Milan was 3–6, and Josh knew they hadn't played most of their games like a 3–6 team. They were crumbling down the stretch, running out of ideas late in games. They had no problems competing; they had problems winning. Randy was there to help, and even though Josh didn't acknowledge the whining about the tie, he could forgive it.

Twenty minutes later, Jeff walked into the office wearing his Milan warm-ups and holding a cream-colored shirt, dark dress pants, and a tie with big orange basketballs on it. He tossed his dress clothes on the worn leather couch in the corner of the office. "A fuckin' tie?" he asked, grinning at both Randy and Josh, thinking he was extending the joke that Randy called him about. Josh shook his head and looked at Randy, then back to the scouting report for Jac-Cen-Del he had pulled out of the file cabinet. Jeff responded by pulling out of his Milan football jacket pocket a pair of black Adidas basketball socks, which he would pass off as dress socks later that night.

Pregame, it was obvious that Josh had as much patience for the team's recent mental performance as he had for Randy and Jeff complaining about wearing a tie to the game that night. His pregame words were simple, tired, pleading. "Go act like you're better than them," Josh said, recalling his disappointment from Wednesday night's game against South Ripley. They should have won that game, Josh knew. Milan was the better team and didn't act like it down the stretch. They didn't have a swagger or confidence in the last minutes. They looked like a team of players who were collectively wondering what would screw things up for them. They became hesitant with the ball and missed free throws. The legendary college coach Skip Prosser used to have his summer campers knock on the hardwood floor each morning. When they knocked, Skip said, "What's that knocking?" The campers, knowing the script, would respond by shouting, "Opportunity!" Skip would tell them over and over: "When opportunity knocks, let it in." Milan was so unaccustomed to a visit from opportunity that when it knocked, the boys seemed to stand behind the drapes in the living room, wondering who the strange presence at the door was, waiting for it to just go away.

Still, Josh pleaded. He was tired, and he told the team so. It wasn't his typical ultra-motivating pumping up—he was subdued. Josh had tried emphatic, and emphatic was three and six for the season.

The Milan fans made up for Josh's quiet pregame. While the gym wasn't packed—seeing as how South Ripley and Batesville were the biggest schools in the county and their fans wouldn't show up for the consolation game before their championship game—it was mostly Milan black and gold. Of the five hundred or so fans in attendance, most were from Milan. It was strange—they didn't turn out for the first-round game, but they did for the consolation game. But that was the difference between a Wednesday 6 p.m. start—right as people were leaving work—and a Saturday evening game.

Not all of the Milan fans were so interested. As Josh walked on the court during pregame, he saw Brad Voss's young son behind the bench. Unlike Ethan or Braden when they were their young cousin's age, Brad's son was deep into a game on his Nintendo DS. Josh walked up three rows to nudge the boy. "Gotta watch the game now!" Josh said, smiling. The boy took just a moment to consider his surroundings, nonchalantly surveying the two teams warming up on the court. "Well, I'll watch some of it." Josh smiled at Brad and walked down the steps. One more Milan fan to be won over.

At halftime, Josh was out of answers. How could he coach a team that insisted on throwing the ball away so much, he wondered out loud. Jac had sped the game up, charging down the court after every steal. Jac barely ran a set play during the second quarter, they pushed the ball so effectively. Josh knew that Milan would be in trouble if the pace kept up because it just wasn't Milan's style. Josh had been looking for opportunities all season to get a two-point lead and hold the ball, run the stall offense to make the game smaller. They couldn't get ahead if they couldn't hold onto the ball on offense, though. Josh started to massage his face, then looked down at his hands. They were covered in blue ink. With four minutes left in the first half and Milan losing 27–12, Josh drew up a play during a time-out and got so mad at the thought of his team not even being able to make three passes in succession that he started beating the marker against the board in a stabbing motion. He busted the marker and threw it through the players' legs under the bench.

He looked at Randy, Jeff, and Tyler. "You guys got any ideas?" Josh asked, remembering why Randy was standing there. Jeff and Tyler looked at each other. "Hold onto the ball?" Tyler asked, frustrated.

"Is it too much to ask for someone to make a midrange shot? Even attempt one? That's what they're giving us," Josh said. "Everyone wants to dunk the ball. Everyone wants to shoot the three. That's what they show on SportsCenter. Hit a twelve-footer."

Randy suggested a play named Bluegill. Josh nodded. "We'll start the second half with Bluegill, then," Josh said. There wasn't a touch of hope in his voice.

At halftime, Josh stomped into the locker room without a word, took a marker, and wrote "12/31" on the whiteboard. "Thirty-one possessions," Josh said, fake giggling to himself. "Twelve turnovers." Josh laughed some more. "Twelve!" No one looked around the locker room to confirm what they saw—that maybe Josh was going nuts. "Can we hold onto the freaking ball?" Josh yelled, snapping out of it. "Can we do it long enough to run a play?"

Milan ran Bluegill on their first play. It was designed to give Nick Ryan a path to the basket for a layup or, if Ethan's man shaded over to cut that off, an open three-pointer to Ethan. Ethan's man slid down to defend Nick, and Nick passed Ethan the ball. Despite bobbling the ball when he caught it, Ethan continued his shooting motion and missed badly off the rim. Josh sat down in his chair, leaned back, crossed his right leg over his left, and folded his arms. It was frustrating—he was putting his team in the right position to succeed, and they couldn't do it.

With six minutes left in the game, Milan was down eighteen points. The game was essentially over. Josh looked down his bench and met Logan Alloway's eyes. Logan had been dominating at the JV level, scoring twenty points or more in every game. He had the body of a junior high school player, but somehow he was speeding past defenders or faking and pulling up for three. *Why not?* Josh thought. After all, didn't he dress Logan for the county tournament for a reason? Logan was clearly the future of Milan basketball, and it was as good—or poor—a night as any for him to make his debut.

Josh pointed at Logan, then thumbed over his shoulder at the scorers' bench like an umpire calling him out. Logan pulled the man-sized gold Milan shooting shirt off his thin frame and stood up. As he walked to the scorers' bench, he nervously tugged at his jersey and made sure his shorts were down on his waist to make them appear baggy, as if the shorts could look any other way on him. Logan had been on the bench for both games of the Ripley County Tournament, both ugly games. He saw his teammates crash to the ground after loose balls and commit a handful of hard fouls. He saw his teammates fail to dissect defenses and get rushed into quick shots. It made him nervous, made him clutch the loose neck of his jersey as if it had suddenly become a turtleneck. He could beat nearly anyone at a shooting contest, but he was intimidated by the physical play of boys he had never met. The game thus far didn't look like it would flatter Logan—it had spiraled out of control and wasn't the pretty brand of basketball Logan played. At times it looked like they were playing rugby, struggling to maintain possession after rebounds and trying to force jump balls. During the possession before Logan entered the game, on which Jac scored after three offensive rebounds, the ball finally fell through the hoop with two Milan players and one Jac player on the ground.

Logan was just as unproductive as the rest of the team at first. He shied away from rebounding and gave up two points on defense. He spent more time looking down at his feet during dead ball situations than he did looking at his teammates for guidance on where to be. When he picked up his man on defense, Logan stayed flat-footed and bent at the waist rather than using the ready position he was taught—on balls of feet, arms out, butt out, head up. He looked like a boy trying to look cool.

Minutes later, he would look cool in the way Josh hoped he would many more times in the future. Zack Lewis dribbled toward Logan, who was standing right in front of the Milan bench. Zack waited until Logan's man slid over to help guard him, then threw Logan the ball. Without hesitation, Logan caught it with his left hand to the side and his right hand behind the ball—a shooter's grip. As he collected the ball, he stopped hunching over and straightened up. He no longer looked like a scared boy—he looked like a basketball player. He looked like he did on that day in early October, taking on two players at once in street clothes in the Milan gym, shooting the ball, then pulling up his pants. Crossing over, pulling up his pants. Smooth. Swagger. The ball arced high, seemingly so high that it dropped at an acute angle down into the basket, touching no part of the rim as Logan registered his first points in a varsity game. He jogged back on defense, now bouncing on the balls of his feet. He slid over and forced his man into a travel. Two plays later, Logan started in the corner in front of the Milan bench, jogged as if he was cutting along the baseline, and snapped back to the corner just as Alex Layden's bounce pass arrived. Just as quickly as Logan had faked and cut back, his shot was up and through the net, once again with a pure rainbow arc. Josh walked back to his seat, and as he passed Randy, Josh allowed himself a smile. "Some people just got it, Randy," Josh said. "Some people can just play."

Josh and Randy stood outside of the locker room door, listening to the boys talk about anything but basketball as they undressed and took a shower. For the second game in a row, Josh was worrying about how soft his team was. And for the second game in a row, he was doing so as the Batesville clones sauntered past on their way to the court for yet another victory.

"We're nice," Randy said, smiling. He said the way a Sunday school teacher who was complimenting his class might. "We're real nice."

Randy got a little more specific with his diagnosis, which wasn't explicitly requested, but expected. "You know, when Kurtis cuts down to the block and receives a pass, he has to reverse pivot to the basket. These guys have been reverse pivoting since before they were born. I don't know why they aren't doing it now."

Josh suppressed the acid that lurched up his throat and swallowed hard. "He can reverse pivot from the bench. I'm done."

As the bus rolled home to Milan carrying the supreme losers of the Ripley County Tournament, Josh pulled his sock cap low on his head until the edge almost covered his eyes. Every thirty seconds or so, he would look at the players at the back of the bus texting and fake wrestling with each other in their seats. He shook his head and returned to staring at the bus seat in front of him, imagining what parent complaints John Prifogle would pass along this week after losing in the first round to the mediocre South Ripley and getting blown out of the consolation game by the smaller Jac-Cen-Del.

Josh traced the cracks in the vinyl on the seat in front of him as he searched his mental file drawer for a drill or a speech he once heard to make the immature and soft boys in the back of the bus get tough and start winning ugly games, games like the two they lost that week. He thought about what he would say to Kurtis when he told him that he wouldn't start against Rising Sun the next weekend. He thought about what Brian Voss would say when Josh revealed the secret he was keeping, even from Randy and Jeff and Tyler: that when Josh saw how much better Braden was in rowdy games, how much better equipped he was on defense to deal with rougher teams, how Braden didn't have to just rely on his shooting ability like Ethan, it became clear that Braden had earned a spot in the starting lineup. It became clear to Josh that he was going to have to bench the player in Milan to whom basketball—not just basketball but *Milan* basketball—mattered most. It became clear to Josh that not only would Ethan lose his starting role, but he would lose it to his little brother. Josh knew this reality would start a war, even if it was the right thing to do. He looked out the window as the bus passed the Dairy Queen and approached the high school parking lot. How long would he be Milan's coach? How many more times would he pass that Dairy Queen?

In the third quarter of the JV game at Rising Sun, Kurtis motioned to his father to come down to behind the bench where the varsity team was watching the JV game. Kurtis's dad always sat in the top row, away from both groups of parents, groups that grew farther apart physically and emotionally with each Milan loss. As his dad approached, Kurtis smelled the familiar fog of cigarette smoke that permeated even his father's leather jacket. He stood up, turned away from the game, and faced his father, who stood on the seats behind him.

"I want you to know now before you bust a gasket when the starting lineups are announced." Kurtis said, using the same tone he might to tell his father that there was still snow on the ground in January or that he planned on watching television that night. "I'm not starting tonight."

Kurtis's dad smiled a little bit. "Want me to kill him now or later?" he asked, clearly joking. His smile faded only a little bit when he said, "I told you a while ago to stop wimping out and get up and go!" He slapped Kurtis on the back, then hiked up the legs of his jeans to climb the stairs, stepping only on the bleacher seats with his work boots. Kurtis turned to Alex. "Well, he took that better than I thought he would."

If anything, Kurtis was relieved that his dad wasn't too upset. For the remainder of the JV game, he discussed with Alex the merits of coming off the bench. Both boys agreed that there was less pressure because they weren't expected to set the tone of the game from the start; rather, they could just fold themselves into the action. The other team didn't necessarily waste one of their best defenders on bench players either, since their matchups were set by the starting lineup. Kurtis had decided that this would be all right, which was one of the problems Josh had with Kurtis. Josh wanted him to be upset, wanted him to want to win.

Ethan wanted to win, but had a different response to the benching. His team needed something different from him than what he gave as a member of the starting lineup. Instead of starting, he would now be expected to do what his brother had been doing all year: coming off the bench and sparking the offense with his long-range shooting. Ethan knew that if he settled into this role, the minutes would come. Milan would always need scoring, and he could provide that. It was up to him to prove his worth and how many minutes he deserved.

It was the type of attitude that made Josh's pregame speech resonate with Ethan. Josh knew that he couldn't bench last year's leading scorer and rebounder, as well as its off-the-court leader, without doing something to recognize the move's significance. Instead of the approach he had taken the previous games, though—talking explicitly about the game or what they needed to do in the game to win—Josh chose to read something to them. Once the boys were settled in the Rising Sun visitors' locker room, Josh pulled a folded piece of paper out of his front pocket and started reading.

PRIDE

I'm a high school player. I'm a team player. I play with my friends and with some of my enemies, but I respect everyone when it comes to my sport. I know I'm not going to get a multi-million dollar contract to play professionally. I know I may not even get my name in the paper. I play for the love of the game. For the pride and honor, for the blood, sweat, and tears it takes to make the team, to earn the spot, to win the game. I play because I can; I play because I know that my life would be empty without the sport I play. I would have a lack of every-thing my sport gives me . . . integrity, courage, talent, fearlessness, pride, strength, stamina, will, and the heart of a champion. If I didn't play, I would lose a part of me. I'm an athlete. I'm a man. I'm a champion, not because my team always wins, but because when we don't, we learn from our mistakes. We try to fix them, and most of all because we have fun. I have built lifelong friendships and memories because of my being an athlete. I leave everything on the court and continue to push myself. I am never happy with second place, but I have learned to accept it. I have learned to get over and through my anger and be the athlete and player I have always dreamed of being. I don't play for my par-ents, for my family, for my friends; I don't play for my coach or my teachers or my school. I play for myself, but when I'm playing I represent them. It isn't about winning or losing, but I hate to lose. I won't settle for a tie, and I am not satisfied with 100%. To play, you have to sacrifice everything, your body, your time, your sweat, blood, and tears, everything . . . for your team. I am a player, an, athlete and a champion, not because I know what it is like to win, but because I know what it is like to lose. I know what it is like to feel the anger and the pain that comes along with "second best." I have been that man with tears in his eyes, walking out to receive the second place trophy and clapping as the other team, my opponents, receive the first place one. I know what it is like to lose, to win, to want to quit, to want to cry, to not want to get up. I know what it is like to hear the cheers and yells for you. I know what it is like to feel the pressure of everyone on your shoulders, and I know what it is like to choke under that pressure. I know what it means to be an athlete, a true player, and that is why I play. I am an athlete, a champion, a true player.

The boys were fidgety during the speech. They bounced their feet as its rhythm picked up. The speech was cliché but appropriately so for teenagers playing for a basketball team on which an inspirational sports movie was based, and it seemed that the most clichéd parts were the ones that resonated most with the players. The sections that mentioned playing for the love of the game got heads bobbing. When Josh read *I know what it is like to lose, to win, to want to quit, to want to cry, to not want to get up*, he looked at Ethan, the only player on the team willing to make eye contact with him during the speech. Ethan smiled at Josh as if to say, *It's okay that you did what you did. I'm not going anywhere.* The parts of the speech about no guarantees and showing emotion and pride seemed directed at Ethan, even though it wasn't something Ethan necessarily needed.

Perhaps the truest thing about the speech was the part about never playing professionally. The gym at Rising Sun was the least professional setting Milan had played in all year. It was small, only twelve rows of bleachers on either side. On one end of the gym, behind the basket, was a stage used for band concerts and school plays. During the game, the pep band sat on stage, set up like an orchestra instead of a band, in four rainbow-shaped rows. To the right of the stage, near the top of the gym, a cartoon sun winked at the crowd on the scoreboard, which said "Home of the Shiners."

On Milan's second possession, one thing was apparent: Braden Voss would get some looks that night. In order to combat the Rising Sun zone, Milan's goal was to move the ball around often with passes, catching Rising Sun as they tried to double-team. Nick Walter caught a pass at the free throw line from John Herzog, realized he was surrounded by Rising Sun players, and tossed the ball to Braden, who was waiting behind the three-point line. No one was near him as he shot and scored his first three points as a starter.

On Milan's next possession, a similar play gave Braden his second three-pointer. Minutes later, thanks to another three by Braden and layups by both Braden and John, Milan was up 18–7 with two minutes left in the first quarter. After every defensive rebound, Josh—still seated—yelled *Go! Go!* to the boys, encouraging them to push the ball up the court. Josh, it seemed, had abandoned the stalling, slow-it-down offense. And why not? Milan was getting the ball up the court before Rising Sun could set up their zone defense, and Milan was finding open shots all over the court. When Zack Lewis committed two early fouls, it was Alex Layden who came off the bench for him, not Ethan or Kurtis. This was what Josh had envisioned when he installed the new offense over the past week, when he thought about his team without Kurtis or Ethan in the lineup. They would run up the court, get quick baskets. Kurtis and Ethan didn't even bother removing their shooting shirts.

When Kurtis came into the game late in the first quarter, he struggled to make an impact. Instead of folding himself into the game plan that was working so well, spacing himself around the court and letting the ball do all the movement, Kurtis took the ball from the right corner and dribbled around, finally traveling as he tried to move to the basket. When Ethan came in for his brother with fifty seconds left in the first quarter, the Milan fans stood and applauded. It wasn't applause for the senior leader, though; it was applause for his little brother, who had made thirteen of Milan's twenty points, along with two steals. Josh's plan—no matter how Kurtis or Ethan fit into that plan—was working.

Before Josh walked into the locker room, Brad Voss stormed in, giving high fives to all of the players. "Good half, boys, good half," he said, pointing at Braden and slapping Ethan on the back. "Nice shootin', Skim," he said to Braden, smiling. "Nice work, E." Brad gloated, knowing his nephews were leading the Milan charge with twenty-five of the team's thirty-seven points. When Josh walked in, Brad disappeared to the edge of the locker room—he didn't want to appear to overstep his boundaries. Josh's halftime talk wasn't much different than his pregame talk—calm, reserved, laissez faire even. He was happy with how most of the team had adjusted to the new game plan and had no designs on changing things, even if Kurtis was sulking in the corner.

Braden was having too good of a night shooting to let Rising Sun back into the game, as Milan had done with their previous opponents. He added three more three-pointers in the third quarter, and after his eighth of the night, he high-stepped back on defense and brushed his shoulders off the way he had seen Jay Z do time and time again on YouTube. He finally missed his first shot with five minutes left in the third quarter. When Josh subbed him out, he sat down on the bench next to his cousin Alex. "Did you like that?" he asked, referring to his celebration. "I heard some guy yell 'Miss!' and I was just like 'I don't think so.'"

Braden's performance had the team smiling again. With three minutes left in the third quarter, Milan had opened their lead back up to fifteen points. Milan had something they hadn't had all year: swagger.

Kurtis was having trouble finding much to smile about. When he was put in the game, he picked up another set of two quick fouls. He had four fouls and was in danger of fouling out. Josh knew Kurtis wouldn't be able to mentally handle fouling out in the third quarter of a game he hadn't played more than a handful of minutes in and took him out as quickly as he put him in. Kurtis walked past Josh without a word, with a painfully blank expression on his face. It wasn't until Kurtis sat by himself at the end of the bench and punched the open chair between him and Logan that he showed any type of emotion. Ethan had handled his benching with grace, contributing in the smaller way he was now expected to contribute. Kurtis didn't yet know what his role would be on this team, one that now looked just fine without him. When Milan players were subbed out, he didn't stand with the team to give them a high five or pat on the back. He sat on the end of the bench, hands folded, head hung.

Late in the fourth quarter, with Milan up by thirteen points, Josh put Kurtis in again for one last chance. Josh's directions were clear: stall for the rest of the game. Move off the ball and pass to the open man. Kill some clock. And Milan was content to do so. With ten seconds left, Milan had the ball and was up 77–68. Rising Sun was beaten, and they called off their defense, knowing Milan would just hold the ball for the final seconds. As the Rising Sun players started to shake hands with Milan while the final seconds ticked off the clock, Kurtis was holding the ball on the left wing, dribbling out the final seconds. The game tape shot from the top of the Rising Sun bleachers doesn't show what happened next. It doesn't show Kurtis Kimla looking up at the scoreboard, seeing four seconds left, and thinking about that number four: the number of points he had scored that night, none of which came on plays designed for him. It doesn't show Kurtis weaving in and out of his teammates shaking hands with Rising Sun and driving to the lane, extending for a layup. It doesn't show the frustrated player, around whom last year's team was built, making his sixth point and violating an unwritten rule in basketball: when the losing team's defense calls off the dogs in the last seconds, the winning team holds the ball and grants mercy to the losers. It doesn't show the Rising Sun players breaking their handshakes with Zack and Alex and Nick and John to confront Kurtis about his running up the score. It doesn't show Kurtis meeting the Rising Sun players with the same blank stare, the same internally frustrated posture that he had all night. Maybe this was Kurtis's new role: to just look out for himself whenever he could. Whatever Kurtis was thinking—all night, or in those regrettable seconds—it was not appreciated by anyone in the gym.

10

STALLING

January 15: 4–7

Josh had tried to win in the style of the 1954 team—no mistakes, a stall offense, judicious shot selection. It hadn't worked. At the end of the Ripley County Tournament, Josh had complained that the midrange jumper—the same shot Ray Craft and Bobby Plump hit down the stretch to win the state championship—was out of vogue, a lost art. Dunk shots and long shots made the highlight shows, not pull-up jumpers from fifteen feet and accurate foul shooting. And so he had embraced the style of play that he couldn't hold the team back from any longer. Would there be mistakes? Enough for Josh to pull his quarter-inch-long hair out. Mistakes were part of the new plan: push the ball up the court, find quick-hitters on offense, and scramble on defense to get the ball back in a hurry. He had tried to impress on the boys how precious each possession was because there were so few of them in a game, especially for a team that would be overmatched by size and strength in many situations. But the old Milan way hadn't been a viable way to win for many years. Josh was just accepting that fact. The old Milan way worked in 1954 when many schools were small like Milan. Not Muncie Central or the Indianapolis schools—they had always been big. But now they were bigger. The Muncie Central team that Milan beat in the 1954 state championship had an enrollment of 1,662, a giant in the day. True, Muncie Central in 2010 was a smaller school, with an enrollment of 1,158. But they were a smaller school thanks to another large school that opened in 1962: Muncie Southside. Muncie Southside in 2010 had an enrollment of 1,092, meaning Muncie Central would have been an even bigger school in 2010 had that school not opened.

School consolidation meant that high schools had a larger number of students to draw from to complete their teams. Of the twenty-three schools Milan played in 1954, fourteen were extinct by 2010. The rest had added enrollments from the area schools that consolidated into the existing programs—the programs they used to play in 1954. Milan had absorbed schools, too: Sunman High School, for instance, which Milan beat in 1954. But Milan hadn't absorbed as many as some other schools. While Muncie Central in 1954 had been one of the largest schools in the state, with 1,662 students, this enrollment would make them only the forty-fourth largest school in Indiana in 2010. School consolidation—a move made necessary mostly in the 1960s and 1970s because of declining tax dollars—significantly decreased the chance of a school Milan's size making the state championship game in the "all-comers" tournament format that had made Indiana high school basketball relevant and exciting in the twentieth century.

Rural students were traveling to new county high schools, and small community high schools were going under (and with them, the hometown feeling that accompanied high school basketball). From Milan's championship in 1954 until the end of the one-class basketball system in Indiana in 1998, no school with an enrollment of under five hundred students won the state championship. Small schools won only a handful of trophies after Milan in 1954, and the ones that did win all had something in common. Connersville in 1972 was led by Mr. Basketball, Phil Cox. And Scott Skiles, the future NBA player and coach, led "tiny" Plymouth (enrollment nine hundred) to the state championship in 1982. Only Connersville in 1983 won the state championship as a small school with balance, and they were led by the Heineman brothers. Milan's championship in 1954 was correctly dubbed a miracle, not because it hadn't been done before, but because a small school playing balanced team basketball (even one with stars like Bobby Plump or Ray Craft) would never win again.

Milan in 2010 had no such stars. John Herzog was good but surely wasn't even considered a small-college prospect. The Voss boys could shoot but could do little else. And Kurtis had his own flaws. Josh had tried the system that led

Milan to the championship in 1954 because it worked once and seemed to be the only way to win with the collection of decent but not well-rounded players he had at his disposal. Maybe Logan Alloway could be that kind of star at some point, but at his current five feet seven inches, it was unlikely. Still, the boys resisted the team approach. What choice did Josh have with a four and seven record? This fast, flashy style was the wave of the future, or at least the current style.

It's what made Josh's role as coach so frustrating. He was coaching in a community where one of the only downtown storefronts was an underfunded museum celebrating the 1954 state championship team, a museum that most present-day Milan players had never set foot in. The museum served as a reminder of the time when a certain style worked, thrived even. The community remembered—how could it forget? The museum, the banner hanging in the gym, the trophy in the lobby, the scoreboard lit and set to 32–30—it all served as a false reminder that doing things right would produce results. But what was right in 1954 no longer worked in 2010. The disconnect was lost on the people in town. *Many look, but few see,* Josh told the Milan Youth Basketball League participants back in November. *Many hear, but few listen.*

And so Milan would try to speed the game up. It seemed especially ironic to abandon their small-ball mentality that weekend of all weekends. Double weekends—weekends in which Milan had both a Friday and a Saturday night game—were rare, but that double weekend was against two 1A schools, Indiana's lowest enrollment class. Milan, with an enrollment of just 378, was a 2A school. Due to the recent creation of charter schools in bigger cities like Indianapolis, Gary, and Evansville, many of the smaller schools in Indiana, like Milan and those in its conference, were in the second quarter of schools based on enrollment. The state champion in the 1A division in 2010 was Indianapolis Metropolitan, a team without a gym that often practiced in the hallways of their charter school. Rising Sun and the Oldenburg Academy team Milan would face the Saturday after Rising Sun were still small enough to earn a 1A classification.

Oldenburg Academy was a Franciscan school in Oldenburg, a town that promoted itself as the "village of spires." The ride there felt like a trip back in time. After passing through Batesville on State Road 229, the trip north became a labyrinth of winding roads up and down hills into the valley of Oldenburg. On top of a hill outside of town, the boys looked out the bus windows to see the German architecture of a town untouched by the twenty-first century. The bus rolled to a halt inside the campus of the academy and the convent of the Sisters of St. Francis, who operated the academy. The school was built around the gym, with four exits from the gym each releasing fans into the hallways of the school, the few classrooms circling the gym.

The gym itself looked like the one in the movie *Hoosiers.* The smallest gym in Indiana, by capacity and perhaps area, it was lit by only a few caged fluorescent lights. John Harrell's Indiana Basketball website listed the Oldenburg gym at a capacity of 484, but the five rows of bleachers on either side would strain to hold 300, even with toddlers and small children on laps. The small cafeteria just outside the doors of one end of the gym doubled as a lounge where fans could consume cans of pop and nachos served from a small kitchen where during the school day the staff served hot lunches to students. There would be no half-court buzzer beaters for either Oldenburg or Milan that evening—the low ceiling would prevent such prayers. As Braden Voss warmed up before the JV game, his high-arching outside shots barely ducked the wood rafters. After the Oldenburg pep orchestra, the managers, and the parents found seats, there was little room for anyone else. By the time the Milan fans—mostly late-arriving parents and a few students—arrived near the end of the third quarter of the JV game, the gym was standing room only.

The gym was so small that directions from the bench boomed off the walls and instantly gave fans access to the inner workings of the game. The fans were so much a part of the game that it was easy for them to wonder if the coaches' directions were being followed correctly. As Logan Alloway committed his third foul in the first half of the JV game—he was playing in both the JV and varsity games at this point, which was within the IHSAA rules as long as he didn't play more than five quarters per night—his dad called him "Lucy" for his transgressions, and it could be heard from the hallway even though he almost said it under his breath.

Josh's pregame instructions seemed focused on the odd environment. "Part of becoming a winning team is getting stops on the road, in a hostile environment," he told the boys. They were collected in half of the visitors' locker room underneath the gym, and they could hear the ball-bounce and sneaker-chirp of the JV game above them. The visitors' locker room was nothing more than a closet with three rows of freestanding lockers, and while most of the varsity players had chosen lockers in the same row, Kurtis Kimla and Jake White— players who had, because of their waning playing time, started to remove themselves from the usual hum of pregame preparations—had chosen lockers a row over and had to stand against the wall behind Josh as he prepared the team for their game. "The great thing about tonight," Josh said, smiling, not looking behind him at Jake and Kurtis, "is that you play in front of a sellout crowd."

As the team jogged off at halftime to go downstairs to their locker room, Josh pulled Zack Lewis aside. Zack was by no means a scoring leader on the team, but he was the point guard and the football team's quarterback, useful for his leadership rather than his production. Josh put his arm around Zack and, rather than admonish him for his frustrated play, asked him to find Kurtis in the locker room and "get his mind right, encourage him." Kurtis was having the same trouble finding the rhythm of the game that he'd had when he was a starter, and he was starting to mope around the court. It didn't help that Kurtis could hear every sigh and muttered word Josh tried to keep to himself on the bench. On nearly every Oldenburg possession, their coach yelled, "Be solid, do what we do." And at halftime, Oldenburg was pleased by the 15–8 score. That's how they won games: grinding offensive possessions that didn't seem to go anywhere for a minute or so. It made Milan, especially Josh and Kurtis, restless.

With 2:49 left in the third quarter, Milan had crawled within three. A three-point deficit with over ten minutes to play meant the game was wide open. Milan was coming off of a win, and everyone on the team felt like they were building a little bit of momentum. They were close to starting the game over essentially with one quarter to play. One quarter—Milan's best against Oldenburg's best—winner takes the game.

Oldenburg wasn't a bad team. They had beaten South Ripley and Waldron, two teams Milan struggled against. If Milan could face Oldenburg in that rickety old gym and win, it would leave them with their first sweep on a double weekend in seven years, when a Randy Combs–led team did it twice in one season en route to Milan's last postseason win. Milan was at a turning point in their season: a win would give them a two-game winning streak headed into the conference schedule. It would give them five wins halfway through their season, putting them on track to win ten games. Back in 1999, when Milan were surprising regional champions, they won only nine regular-season games. Two games in a row might give the team that winning mentality Josh had been searching for all along.

Josh thought it would help if Kurtis started playing his game. The matchup against Oldenburg seemed created just for Kurtis. Oldenburg's zone had erased Braden's outside shooting (he would end up just one for twelve on the night), and Ethan had been accurate but received few open looks. The Milan offense needed strength, someone to take on two defenders in a more direct manner. That was Kurtis's game—being more physically gifted than his defender, not being denied. It was what made him a star last year, and getting away from that style was what made him a fringe player thus far in his junior year. Josh let him know, in a way that Zack wasn't able to at halftime, that Kurtis could win this game for Milan if he would stop his pouting (*take that towel off your head and get your head up!*) and get physical.

On Milan's first possession, Kurtis received a pass in the corner and lowered his shoulder in a way that let the Oldenburg defenders know they didn't want to be on the receiving end. He was fouled on the arm as he extended to lay the ball in, and made one of his two free throws. Twice on defense, he followed his man high to nearly half-court, denying a pass and forcing Oldenburg to deviate from their set play. The first time Kurtis touched the ball again on the offensive end, he put his head down and drove. He was fouled before he could shoot, but since the referees had been so picky all night, Milan was in the bonus. Kurtis received the ball at the free throw line, bounced it once, and shot it too hard off the back of the rim. Too aggressive. Josh spun away from the court; out of the corner of Kurtis's eye, he saw Josh flipping his dry-erase marker in the air. Kurtis was finally doing the things Milan needed him to do, but he was too pumped up to hit his free throws.

Even though Kurtis rarely showed it through posture or word, he wanted nothing more than to regain his standing with Josh, to once again be the scoring leader of the Milan team. That's what all those sideways glances and towel-over-the-head pouting sessions were about—not about a player playing for himself, but about a player who desperately wanted to play for the team. He just didn't express himself in the same way as Ethan or any of the other guys. So when Kurtis hit a three-pointer—a rare attempt for him—with four minutes left to cut the score to 28–24, when Josh slapped him on the ass after he called time-out and yelled, loud enough for the student workers in the cafeteria next door to hear, "That's the Kurtis Kimla I know!," he smiled a bit. The fourth quarter until that point had been the Kurtis Kimla Show, for all its ups and downs and missed free throws and passionate drives to the basket. Passionate drives? It wasn't something Kurtis had shown all year. Josh was starting to think that Kurtis was finding his form.

Ethan was doing his best to keep Josh's attention as well. After Oldenburg made two free throws to keep the lead at six, Ethan halved it with a three-pointer, thanks to an offensive rebound and pass from Kurtis. Kurtis, instead of smiling as he ran to the huddle for a time-out, looked up at his dad and put his hand to his brow, extending his arm in a salute. He hadn't made the three, but he had made the three happen. He had made *something* happen when it had been so long since he had been a factor for Milan.

The first three quarters and a half had been the longest all year. The clock was pushing 9 p.m. when Kurtis passed to Ethan for that three-pointer. The referees had extended the length of the game, calling fourteen fouls in the third quarter alone. Oldenburg was in the double bonus with a little over three minutes remaining, meaning any foul—and there were sure to be many—would result in two free throws. Milan was in the bonus, meaning nonshooting fouls would result in a one-and-one free throw opportunity—hit the first, get a second. It was becoming clear that this game would be won at the free throw line, the same line that had plagued Milan all season, the same line that represented all the missed opportunities in Milan's season thus far. The same line that, when Milan was at its best in the 1950s, it had dominated from. Fewer chances meant Milan had to be perfect.

Kurtis was clearly fouled on a missed layup, and Josh stomped down the court after an official when the foul wasn't called. Milan was only down six—a deficit that could have been cut to four if Kurtis had received and made the free throws he was entitled to. Those free throws could have meant a tie game if Milan hit them.

In the end, the missed call didn't matter, because Milan couldn't concentrate and slow down at the line to take the few chances afforded them. After Kurtis hit a layup to cut the score to 43–36 with 1.6 seconds left, Josh called time-out. The call brought boos from the Oldenburg crowd—it had already been a long game, and there was no way Milan could win with under two seconds left, but Josh couldn't let it go. He wanted to prove his point. He sat everyone down and pointed at the scoreboard. "This game was ours, guys," he yelled over the boos. "And because we can't hit free throws, we gave it away. I can't shoot them for you."

Josh walked off the court before the final horn sounded. As Oldenburg inbounded the ball, Braden stole it and heaved a three-quarters-of-the-court-length shot that hit the low roof. Milan had lost to Oldenburg by seven points. They had missed nine free throws, shooting a mere seven of sixteen. They missed three front ends of one-and-ones, meaning they should have had three more free throw attempts. Twelve missed opportunities for points, and a seven-point deficit.

When Josh entered the locker room, he stopped at the doorway for a moment. Alex Layden had taken control of what originally was the quietest locker room yet. He sat on the bench choking over his tears, about to throw up from the mix of sweat and tears rolling into his opened mouth. He had committed a flagrant foul down the stretch that hadn't hurt the team that much—Oldenburg missed both free throws—but it hadn't helped, since Oldenburg got to keep the ball. Alex Layden wasn't the reason Milan lost—he hadn't attempted any shots, because that wasn't his role on the team. That didn't mean that he didn't want to win as much as his cousin Braden, who had missed eleven three-pointers that night, or his cousin Ethan, who had picked up as much of the slack for Braden as he could have, or Kurtis, who finally decided to attack instead of sit back and play passively. "I couldn't ask more from you," Alex said, gasping for air through his tears. He knew that this was a game Milan should have won if they were going to be the team they thought they could be, a team that could challenge in the conference and maybe win a postseason game or two. "I hope you couldn't ask more from me." It was Alex who had originally started their pregame cheer, a cheer that had lost steam during the losing streak.

Josh had little to say to the team after the game because Alex had said it all—they needed to stop worrying about Josh. Kurtis needed to stop searching out Josh's reaction after something went wrong. They needed to start playing for themselves, the team, the town. *We ask for a chance that's fair.* Milan needed to focus on the small matter of capitalizing on those chances. The conference season was coming: their first conference game was nine days away. They had nine days to prepare for South Ripley, and then they would play a double weekend against Southwestern and Switzerland County. They had nine days to forget Oldenburg and somehow recover that ethereal memory of winning, a memory that seemed weeks in the past instead of hours.

In the moldy locker room beneath the smallest high school gym in Indiana, it was clear that hard work wasn't enough sometimes. Sometimes a team needed a break. Sometimes a team needed a bit of skill. Sometimes a team needed an identity like Oldenburg's to rally around. Milan wasn't getting much of those three things, hadn't for almost ten years. Nine days would be the biggest gap between games in Milan's season, but it also seemed like less time than Milan needed to fix their problems. Their problems ran deep; they started when the baskets hung on barn walls and in driveways started to rust. They started when the nets that were torn down by the cold winter wind weren't replaced when the sun came out in March. They started when the family farms were sold and the town elevator's stockpile dwindled. All across eastern Ripley County, free throws were being missed. Teachers were being laid off. Coaching pay was being cut by 50 percent. It wasn't hard to see how things were matching up on the court. Oldenburg was a small school, but as a private school, it was small by design. It wasn't hard to see the harder life in Milan reflected in the harder times for the team. It wasn't hard to see that no matter how much Milan pushed the ball up the court, they were still stalling, just hoping to hold onto the ball. Stalling, just hoping to make the game small in a way it might never be again.

11

AGAIN

Conference Season: 4–9

It seemed lately that the only thing Josh could predict was when his ear would drain. He would keep his black-and-gold sock cap on as long as he could without looking unprofessional to keep air from swirling into his ear canal and irritating his middle ear, the part that throbbed with every stressful thought or movement. It was about this stage in the schedule during the previous year when Josh visited the specialist in Cincinnati about his other ear. Surgery was planned the day of last game of the season. Just as in the current year, Milan was coming off of losses to Oldenburg and South Ripley and was searching for answers. This year's team was better, which made the losses even more frustrating.

Josh had gone ahead with the surgery on the day of the last regular-season game of 2009–10 because it didn't make much difference whether he was on the sidelines or not; Milan was in the middle of a losing streak that would stack up to ten straight losses by the end of the season. It had been a frustrating first year of head coaching, and Josh thought maybe getting someone else on the sidelines for one night might change things around. It didn't.

Basketball was Josh's reason for being a teacher, the reason he fought through the ear problems to spend long days in a windowless office. Basketball was a release from stress. Josh and Jill had been trying to have a child for several years without any luck. They had started trying in the fall and winter, hoping that a baby would be born in the off-season. A year or two later, and the timing no longer mattered. Jill was a few years older than Josh. Timing? They were running out of time to worry about timing.

Once, basketball had been a release for Josh. Now, it seemed to cause stress. On the team's January 28 game against Southwestern, Josh started the game confident because he knew they could beat Southwestern—they had done just that a month ago across town at Hanover College. Josh allowed the boys some confidence too. He didn't mind when they made a show of their pregame chest bumps in the middle of the court. He clapped emphatically as Milan methodically worked to get three straight layups to open the game.

They had trouble capitalizing on their quick offensive start, but at halftime Milan was down by only four points. And for once Josh didn't have to worry about how to motivate the team to hit their free throws. After the previous several games' free throw woes, Josh had made an even bigger point in the week's practices about the importance of making their shots when the clock was stopped. Each player shot 160 free throws in practice that week, and the free throws were keeping Milan in the game at halftime.

Milan didn't let the game go. Late in the third quarter, John Herzog dribbled through the defense and was fouled hard as he shot a layup, landing flush on his side under the basket. The sound of him hitting the court echoed off the walls of the gym. Josh wouldn't blame him a bit for coming out of the game after the hit, but he limped to the line to take his free throws. Minutes later, John was fouled hard again shooting a layup to open the fourth quarter. As John collected himself from the floor and struggled to walk to the free throw line, Josh turned to look at Jeff and smiled. "That's a tough kid right there," Josh said. Despite John's toughness—toughness he had shown all season—Milan never got back within four points of Southwestern and lost by seven.

After the bus pulled into Milan's parking lot around 10:30, Jeff and Tyler knew they were in for a long night. Josh didn't say much on the bus on the way home, and when he was quiet, he was ready to break down film looking for answers. They had installed a new offense that wasn't producing any better results than the old offense. They shot free throws all week at practice, and it worked, but it wasn't enough to win. All Josh said on the bus home was: "I hate my life. Hate it, hate it, hate it. Hate it for them." He nodded back to the guys like Zack and

John and Ethan and Braden who were playing their hardest and not finding the results they felt they deserved.

The film session the coaches held in their office after the game stretched until 1 a.m. and didn't provide relief or answers. All it did was extend their frustration, made them relive all the silly mistakes. And that's why they were losing games. It wasn't the scheme, it wasn't the lineup, it wasn't the effort. It was things like bobbling a ball or running a play incorrectly. It was hard to tell whether the film session was a therapeutic chance to let their anger out or an unhelpful rehash of problems the adults were unable to fix.

Josh wasn't just worried about watching the game that had ended three hours earlier. "We're just one game better than last year," Josh said through a yawn. Last year the team had achieved all of their three wins by January 15, then ended the year with ten straight losses. Josh wondered if the same thing could happen this year, if the four games they had already won would be their last of the season. "We gotta be doing something wrong," he said, taking the last pull from his Diet Mountain Dew can. It was a question he would be asking himself until he pulled into his driveway at nearly 2 a.m.

Josh had intended to wake up at 8 a.m. but allowed himself a few snooze cycles and took twenty extra minutes of sleep. He was dreading the Saturday for a few reasons. The Southwestern loss had played in his head all night and made for restless sleep. Saturday wouldn't be much easier. That night he would face off against his friend and former colleague, B.J. McAllister. But before Milan faced Switzerland County at home after a grueling loss, Josh had to deal with the Milan alumni and their annual game in the Milan gym.

As Josh sat on his couch watching the morning news, Jill fixed him a travel mug of coffee. He struggled to pull on his tennis shoes through the early-morning body stiffness. He yawned, then in a mocking tone looked over his shoulder at Jill and said, "Welp, another fun-filled alumni game." He paused for a moment, watching the weather for ice or snow or blizzard, something to get him out of the alumni game. Instead the weather was supposed to be unseasonably warm for January 29. "How's the team, coach?" Josh continued to mock. Not only did Josh have the alumni game and a conference game on his mind, but he had an early-morning practice to run with the team. He needed a way to get them thinking they could challenge Switzerland County. Josh had been looking forward to coaching against B.J. all winter.

"I'm just glad you guys lost last night," Jill said, setting Josh's travel mug next to him on the end table. She hadn't been able to attend the game because she had a late shift at the hospital the previous night, meaning neither Josh nor Jill had gotten much sleep. "Last time I missed a game you guys won."

Josh stopped in Batesville at the Subway to pick up an egg sandwich and an orange juice. Both were consumed by the time his pickup truck reached the used car lot on the west side of Milan. The junior high and freshman teams were wrapping up their practice. Josh noticed a woman in the bleachers, and before going to his office to hang up his jacket or prepare for practice, he knew he needed to talk to her. She was there to pick up her freshman son from practice.

"I heard about the game the other night," Josh said.

The woman smiled. She knew Josh wasn't talking about the freshman basketball game her son played in, but the fifth-grade game her twin sons played in the previous week. Milan was playing in a schoolboy league in Madison, forty-five minutes south, because the youth league didn't have enough support to hold games.

"Twenty points and nineteen," the woman said with a chuckle. Josh was used to talking to the parents of the younger players in town on Wednesday nights when the Milan Youth Basketball League met to run the town's grade schoolers through drills. The moms would talk to Josh about how much their sons loved basketball, but always with an apologetic look. Another guard, coach. Another kid that might hit six feet if he's lucky. The woman knew she didn't need to apologize for her twins, who were wrestling in the lobby of the gym and almost sweating through their matching Indianapolis Colts winter coats.

"Whole fifth-grade teams don't score twenty or nineteen," Josh said.

"I know," she said. "You ready to have 'em on your team?" The question seemed to be a combination brag and plea to get the rambunctious eleven-year-olds out of her hair.

"Hell, don't know if I'll be around that long," Josh said.

In practice, Josh gave each of the JV players roles to play to mimic Switzerland County. "This is 'Pacer,' guys. This is their big set." Josh directed the JV team through the play.

"Look familiar to anyone?" Josh asked. The boys looked down at their shoes, not wanting to meet Josh's eyes.

"It's our 'catfish,'" Josh said, not wanting the embarrassing silence to last any longer. It was no surprise that Josh and B.J. had the same plays, since they coached together at New Albany. Jill had tried to avoid the topic that morning. Josh and B.J. had the same philosophy, the same plays, the same motivational tactics. The game would come down to the little things, to individual players performing, to execution. Josh would know exactly what B.J. was trying to do, and B.J. would know what defenses to call when Josh called out his plays. For every Pacer, there was a Catfish.

"I do not want to get beat on the stupid little Purdue cuts we beat people with!" Josh yelled as he moved a JV player through a Switzerland County play.

As the boys ended practice with more free throws, Josh walked around the court and kicked up pieces of the floor sealant that had bubbled and chipped. He knew he had a group of the program's biggest critics playing on the court in just a few hours and didn't want them to have anything to complain about. Jeff commented that he heard the new superintendent was in favor of putting in a new floor in about two years, which was surprising, since the basketball team lost funding for an assistant coach that year, and Josh's stipend was cut from $6,000 to $3,000.

"Hell, when that happens, you'll never be able to get in here to play," Jeff said. "They'll have combination locks on the doors, lasers on the floor like a spy movie." Josh thought about what that might mean to the boys in town who might be on his team one day. The driveway hoops were disappearing, and the small town park didn't have a court anymore—it was taken out by the town council, who cited vague safety reasons. The coaches had wanted to put a couple of goals up in the school parking lot, but the request was denied because there wouldn't be a fence up to prevent cars from hitting players on the court. The coaches were frustrated because that seemed an unlikely scenario, especially since in the summer you could count the number of cars that drove through the Milan High School parking lot in one day on two hands. Josh thought about those twin fifth-graders who scored all those points this week, thought about what they would do when the season ended. He tried to picture their house— Did they have a hoop in their driveway? Where would they go for hours to shoot? Jeff was just joking—just like when he caught the Voss boys leaving practice and told them that he was playing in the alumni game in a few hours, so if they wanted to bring notepads they might learn something—but it seemed to worry Josh. How would he provide kids in town access to basketball, the same access that all the alumni who were about to play on the court had when they were kids? How would those kids get the practice, the love of the game, the repetition of shots from the corner and the free throw line that put Milan on the map those years ago? Josh kicked up a piece of sealant from the painting of the state of Indiana at center court. He paused and looked at the gym floor. "The Heart of Hoosier Hysteria," Josh read to himself. How could he make that true again?

12

SOMETHING POSITIVE

Alumni Weekend: 4–10

Josh had passed responsibility for the alumni game off on Jeff Stutler. Jeff would be playing, Jeff knew the players, and ultimately Josh didn't want to bother with the game. Milan no longer had a homecoming game for basketball, just football. The alumni game was close enough—there would be two games in the afternoon, then everyone would grab a bite to eat at their parents' house or with their families if they still lived in town and come back to watch the high school game that night. The younger alumni—guys still in their twenties—were scattered around southeastern Indiana or Cincinnati. Some were going to school; some were working factory jobs in Batesville or Lawrenceburg.

Part of the reason Josh passed the responsibility off on Jeff was because the alumni game stressed him out. The alumni wanted to come back and play, wanted to relive their time in the black and gold. Reliving meant telling tall tales of 90-percent-from-the-field shooting nights and towering dunks. Josh didn't mind running the golf scramble in the summer for the 1954 team—it raised money for the team jerseys, those guys were great to be around (their tall tales were usually true), and it was in the summer when Josh wasn't spending twelve hours a day preparing for the next basketball game. When he was spending that kind of time and energy—time and energy spent away from his wife, whose reminders about her desire to start a family were starting to become more frequent—some thirty-year-old talking about how dominant Milan used to be and offering suggestions wasn't Josh's idea of a good time.

Forty-five minutes before the game was supposed to start, nearly two-thirds of the men playing in the game were on the court warming up. On the end nearest the parking lot were the men older than thirty-five, who would play in the first game. Opposite them, the younger men gathered. The men on each side of the court rarely mixed—every now and then Jeff Stutler or John Prifogle would see a former student or player he especially liked or hadn't seen in a while and cross over to the young side to catch up a bit.

The sides' contrast in style was telling. At one point about thirty minutes before the game was supposed to start, the younger men stopped shooting. The only black man in the gym, a hulking man named Bryant Withers, palmed a ball behind the three-point line. He wore a red cutoff shirt and Air Jordan shoes. The shoes were still the bright, almost-neon white they were the first day he bought them, but you could tell they had been well used at the YMCA in Batesville. Many of the men, as you would expect, were not in the shape they were in in high school. Withers, palming the ball on the perimeter, must have been in better shape than he was five years ago—no eighteen-year-old could have the shoulders and biceps he sported. He smiled at the crowd that had collected behind him, clearing the lane. The corners of his mouth seemed to reach toward his diamond stud earrings. The younger men joked with him for a bit—they all wore shorts that extended past their kneecaps, and most had visible tattoos on their arms and calves. Withers bounced the ball once and, like a long jumper, bounded toward the basket, timing his final leap to be just a yard or two inside the free throw line. He extended the ball like the Michael Jordan silhouette embroidered on his shoes and stuffed it into the basket, violently pulling the rim down and letting it pop back up with the loud creak of metal straining against metal. The younger men joked, and some of the shorter men mimicked the dunk, only to finger roll the ball up and through the hoop at the last minute when they jumped a foot or more too low.

The men on the other side of the gym were just twenty feet away, but they acted twenty worlds away. They somehow missed Bryant Withers's little show, missed the "Oh!" chorus from the young men watching when he dunked, missed the thump of the breakaway rim snapping back into place. They were busy shooting free throws, tossing the ball in the air with backspin to simulate a pass, and practicing their three-point shooting rhythm. The older men who weren't taking their warm-up shooting seriously were lifting their children up to shoot layups or catching up with old friends. Most of the older men had crew cuts and tucked their T-shirts into gym shorts that extended to just above the knee-cap. Once the dunk show was over, the young men starting practicing their shooting too, but made about a quarter of the shots the older men made.

After thirty-six alumni had collected—seventeen of them "old-timers"—the older men played their game. They played sixteen-minute halves with a running clock. As they played, Randy Combs narrated the game from the scorers' bench microphone. His narration was mostly for the pleasure of those playing, since the only nonplayers were a couple of small children and Linda White Baurley, who was there to pass out Milan '54 Museum brochures. She hadn't had much luck with the younger crowd of men, but she hoped that if she could catch some of the older men after their game, they might stop by the museum and even donate. Linda clapped politely when David Voss—Braden, Ethan, and Alex's uncle—drained a three-pointer, which prompted Randy to shout, "That's Mister! Ripley! County! Nineteen eighty-five!" into the microphone.

Hours later, Josh was finally alone for a few moments. He had plenty to think about: Milan hadn't managed a win at home all year, and now they were playing in front of the handful of alumni who stayed in town after the alumni game. When Josh passed through the gym after the JV game, he saw them sitting directly across the floor from the home bench in the first row of the bleachers. The group was mostly alumni from the past five years. They watched the varsity team warm up in silence, leaning forward and resting their folded hands in between their knees. The way they sat made them look like coaches, every one of them.

Josh rubbed his eyes. More coaches in the crowd was the last thing he needed. It seemed like a weekly occurrence now that John would come into his office, sit down on the cracked leather of the couch, and start a conversation with "I don't want you to worry, but," or "I'm taking care of it, but." It would be best if Josh just let him take care of it, John would say. And John was probably right. John had lived in Milan all his life and knew the ins and outs of local politics better than Josh. He knew what the Walters wanted because he'd known them for years. He knew what Russell Pitts and his father wanted. He knew what John Herzog's dad was complaining about. Each of them wanted a bit of the past in their present. The Walters wanted their son Nick to play more, to make all his time practicing and traveling to games and away from his studies mean something. Russell Pitts and his dad wanted Josh to take it a little easier on Russell, give him more playing time at the JV level. John Herzog's dad didn't care about any of the stuff off the court; he just wanted Josh to engineer a win once in a while. He had his own ideas of how that might happen—playing John at the point rather than the off-guard for starters, but to generally be more positive when things were going well would work too—and he was starting to voice those ideas from the crowd.

All along, Josh had tried to keep his message to the team consistent. They were "returning to glory," Josh told the team. They were going to state soon. They'd do it a certain way—at first they'd do it with tough defense and long offensive possessions, then Josh thought they'd speed the game up. Now they were back to slowing the game down again. It was what worked for the state title, with the same type of team full of guards. It would be what worked for Milan now.

The voices around town and in the stands were threatening that solidarity. Josh had no reason to believe that Nick or John would start listening to their parents and lose faith in their coach. At selective moments, Josh would pull one of them aside and encourage them, making sure they were still with him. They were, although it was unclear why. The junior class had a unique bond, and it was made stronger with Ethan's benching and Braden's ascendance to a starting spot. The juniors had played together all their lives and had experienced some measure of success. The senior class had never experienced a winning season at any level, not even as grade schoolers. John and Nick might have been playing for their classmates more than for Josh, but that didn't matter. What mattered was that they were a group, despite what was happening around them.

Josh knew winning would solve or at least overshadow these problems. He hoped that night would be the beginning of the solution. The voices in the crowd were becoming more distinct and more personal—targeted directly at Josh rather than at the team, making orders for Josh rather than generally grumbling. Jill was off work that night and would be in the stands. She knew all about the problems and would pick a less conspicuous seat in the gym as a result. Josh's parents and grandparents were coming that night too, and so Jill would usher them to a spot along the far wall, far away from John Herzog's dad's new favorite spot eight rows behind the bench, and far enough away from the Walters, who sat fifteen rows up from the visitors' bench, whispering under their breath at every transgression. B.J. would be too wrapped up in the game to hear anything, so Josh wouldn't be embarrassed by what B.J. heard or didn't hear. As always,

Josh expected to not hear a thing. He expected to beat B.J. and Switzerland County and start a run that would take Milan through the tournament.

Josh had one thing to comfort him while he was looking at scores and worrying about his game that night: the junior varsity team had everyone believing that beating Switzerland County would be possible. The JV team's performance had mirrored the varsity team's so far, which is to say they were outmatched in most games and lost the others through their own mistakes.

Jeff walked into the coaches' office after the JV win and broke Josh's silence. "He finished with thirty-three," Jeff said with a smile, knowing he didn't have to define the pronoun for Josh. "We finally got one."

Josh smiled. "So I gotta tell you something, Jeff. I just talked to B.J." According to Josh, at Switzerland County's walkthrough that morning, B.J. overheard Coach Boggs (the JV coach) talking about how he was going to run a box-and-one defense on Logan Alloway. B.J. had said that he told Boggs that under no circumstances would he run a box-and-one in a JV game. "B.J. said Boggs pouted all the way to Milan on the bus," Josh said.

Jeff grinned wider than he had for three months. With his slow drawl, Jeff said, "I'm gonna go talk to Boggs and say 'Geez, he had thirty-three freaking points, you shoulda box-and-oned him!'"

Fifteen minutes later, the joke and the good feelings had disappeared in the hallway behind the home bleachers. When Josh, Jeff, and Tyler swung the door to the boys' locker room open, they did so with grave purpose. Josh listed most of the reasons the boys needed to sacrifice all of themselves to win the game that night: they were 0–4 at home that season, they were playing in front of their alumni, and Switzerland County was a conference and sectional opponent. Milan needed to take the upper hand for once, and the time had come, according to Josh. Even with the parental pressure on his mind, he delivered that message by saying, "This losing at home shit needs to stop. This losing to conference and sectional opponents crap needs to stop."

When the boys were done with their pregame ritual, Josh tried to create an atmosphere of urgency by slapping each boy on his ass and saying, "Let's go, let's get out there." When Josh got to Zack Lewis, he was starting to turn to the bathroom rather than the door.

"Let's go, Zack, big game," Josh said.

"I gotta pee, man," Zack said, unwilling to get himself too excited.

"Then go pee," Josh said, shaking his head. Every time Josh tried to position a game as the biggest yet, something—even something little—seemed to undermine him.

Josh allowed himself a little smirk. He had so much riding on this game. He and Jill were trying to build a life together—a family soon, they hoped. Jill had a good job as a nurse at the hospital in Shelbyville, but Josh had only seven wins in two years, and now there was a group of parents complaining to John Prifogle. There were rumors that they were holding meetings at the VFW and in homes, strategizing on how to get Josh fired. He'd end that year with two years of head coaching experience. Milan was no longer considered a premier job—hadn't been for decades—so how would he move up or even laterally if he lost his job? Around Indiana, school corporations were laying off teachers, not hiring. They especially weren't hiring basketball coaches who won a third of their games or less, coaches who were run out of town by players' parents. Athletic programs in Indiana were a small fraternity, especially in boys' basketball. People would know. Jill desperately wanted a child. Josh, too. But Josh also wanted a way to provide for that child, and coaching basketball was the only thing he'd focused on since he coached the freshman team at Anderson High School during his sophomore year at Ball State. Josh was hoping to best his former colleague at New Albany, the guy he learned the ropes with. That would mean something to him, would be a very personal achievement. Josh's ears had been throbbing since Thursday. All Zack Lewis wanted to do was take a piss.

The mood was tense in the Milan gym. During the announcement of the starting lineups, the boys stared at the floor, their eyes not following the spotlight searching the dark gymnasium. Josh sat at the end of the bench, rubbing the back of his buzz cut nervously. Both Josh and the boys bounced their legs to the bass drum line of the tomahawk chop.

Josh was too excited to speak in the huddle between quarters. His hands shook so much that he was having difficulty hanging onto the marker. Coaching against B.J. was difficult because Josh knew what B.J. was likely to do. Instead of just worrying about his own team, Josh had to think about what B.J. might call and then run through his mental catalogue of plays to select a play to best combat B.J.'s call.

"I was going to run Mississippi State but that won't work," Josh yelled over the pep band. He stalled—he had forgotten what play he was going to call.

"What about Louisville?" Zack said—more of a command than a question, with time running out for Josh to draw up a play.

Josh snapped his fingers at Zack. "Yes, that's it."

At halftime, Josh tried to calm himself and the team down. They were up three points, but no Milan lead ever seemed safe.

"Good half, but let's get something straight," Josh said, pacing in front of the boys at their lockers. "At no point in time is one pass and a contested shot good offensive basketball. Not in these United States of America. Nowhere."

Josh loved to joke with the boys using these types of hyperbolic statements. Milan looked nervous. They needed to relax a bit. After Josh made sure one or two of the boys at least smirked a bit, he told them that the first three minutes of the second half would be vital. "Think of it as the most important three minutes of your life," Josh said. After a moment, he added, "Well, right now anyway."

But after three minutes in the second half, Switz's Trevor Smith had attempted and made two three-pointers. That's when the wheels came off for Milan. Kurtis Kimla forced a drive to the basket and was called for an offensive foul. John Herzog picked up his third foul on a three-point play for Switz. Milan ran a play for Kurtis, and he forced a quick shot. Josh called a time-out when the score was pushed to 30–18, seemingly just to let the boys watch him smack a water bottle down the bleachers, getting the managers wet.

John Herzog's dad couldn't stay silent any more. As the next play took too much time to develop, he stomped his foot on the wood bleacher in front of him. As the Milan players ran into each other cutting and setting screens, he stood up and yelled, "Come on!" Josh did his best to block out the noise from the stands, but it was hard to ignore John's dad—one of the tallest men in the gym, seven rows behind the home bench. Making it harder to ignore was just how out of character it was for John's dad. Josh pressed on, urging his team to stay tight on defense. It would be Milan's only hope.

Kurtis was once again the unlikely source of steadiness for Milan. With five minutes left in the game, Josh called a time-out with Milan down just seven. Kurtis had methodically worked around in the lane to claw Milan back, and Braden scored a three-point play when he stole the ball and took the shot right at Switz's six-foot-five center, Alex Curran, making the layup while being fouled. Josh collected the boys on the bench, then slammed the marker-board down on the floor. "Every time we draw one up, you guys get tight," Josh said. He looked at Kurtis. "Has anyone stopped you all night?" Kurtis shook his head no. Josh was emphatic—he wanted to get the team believing in Kurtis and that they could finish this comeback off. To the outsider, it looked like Josh was yelling, but he was just fired up. John's dad cupped his hands around his mouth and yelled, "How about something positive in there?" so the whole gym could hear. "Go score," Josh said as he poked Kurtis in the shoulder. "Just go score." As the boys jogged back on the court, Josh turned and looked at Jeff. "I got a lot of positives," Josh said.

In the end, it wasn't enough. Kurtis had his best night perhaps all year, but the third quarter was too much to compensate for. Down the stretch, Milan got within five or seven points, but B.J. would know what play was coming from Milan and have the perfect defense called. John Herzog's dad stood up at the horn and said, "There we go. We lost again." Meanwhile, B.J. was telling Josh, "I know you don't want to hear this, but you did exactly what you were supposed to do, and we made some horseshit shots." As Josh kicked open the door to his office, saying, "It's official, we have found every way to lose a game ever," John Herzog's dad made his way over to the other young alumni, asking what they thought of the game, rolling his eyes.

In the locker room, it was clear that the boys took the loss hard. They were running out of games at home, and winning in front of their alumni would have meant a lot. They wanted to win for Josh too, since they knew he and B.J. were friends and they had watched a movie at his house during the holiday tournament. Kurtis and Braden were crying into gym towels as Josh walked in.

It's a good thing Josh kicked the door on his way into his office, or he might have been tempted to let his anger out on the team. After all, the third-quarter fiasco wasn't a new one—for some reason the team was performing poorly in every third quarter. They would get so close by halftime, only to let it all slip away. Maybe they weren't ready to play after the half. Maybe they started imagining a win and weren't mentally tough enough to stay focused. Josh had his theories about the team's mental toughness, and they weren't good theories. But as he saw emotion from Kurtis for the first time in a while, Josh knew he could save the complaining for another day.

"There's nothing you could have done differently," Josh said, seemingly speaking only to Kurtis. "You did everything defensively you were supposed to do."

Later, in Josh's office, Coach Sharp, one of the football coaches, stopped in to offer some advice. "Hell, let 'em foul out. Run the secondary break more." Josh did his best to not respond. "It's been the same damn game for ten games in a row," Sharp said. Seeing that Josh wasn't in the mood to have a conversation about strategy at that moment, Sharp turned his attention to Stutler. "You goin' to the club with the alumni tonight, Stut?"

Jeff looked briefly at Josh, as if he thought for a moment it would be best if he asked permission from the man nearly thirty years his junior.

"Yeah," Jeff said.

"They'll be full of answers," Sharp said, perhaps trying to deflect from the answer session he just had of his own.

"Hell, I'm the smart guy tonight," Jeff said, smiling at Sharp and Randy, who had just walked in.

"Shit," Randy said. "I'm not going to listen to that stuff."

Once Randy, Jeff, and Sharp departed for the country club, that left just Josh in his office, shirtless, with his dress pants still on. Jill knocked softly on the door frame and walked in, with Josh's parents and grandparents behind her. Josh looked at them and shook his head, an annoyed scowl on his face. His grandmother walked over and kissed his head.

"You'll win," she said to him, knowing that he was unhappy about the game, not about seeing them.

"Not with this team," Josh said.

13

SITTING TOGETHER

February 10: 4–12

Josh had problems, and he wanted to make sure he knew what they all were. Some were made evident to him. Brian Voss spent forty-five minutes on the phone with Josh, complaining about how he thought Josh was mistreating Ethan. Ethan played fourteen minutes in the loss to Switzerland County, and in the game after it—a thirteen-point loss to Rising Sun, a team they beat handily three weeks prior—Ethan played only seven minutes. Ethan wasn't going to complain even if it wasn't the way he imagined his senior season. Ethan may have been the only player who seemed to think it was just a bit special to play basketball for Milan High School, but poor defense and a cold shooting streak had relegated him to Josh's bench. Ethan knew why he was being used less, and he worked hard in practice to regain Josh's trust. But Brian knew Ethan had dreamed of leading this team during his senior season, ever since he played on his Papaw Hank's backyard court, when Braden, Alex, and Ethan begged Papaw Hank to not park his Milan School Corporation bus on the concrete slab so they could play until dinnertime. Brian also knew that Ethan would never say a word about how much it disappointed him that he couldn't figure prominently in Josh's plans. So Brian called.

Then there were the accusations that he had to discuss with the superintendent and the five members of the school board, which included Zack Lewis's dad, Greg. The parent group, led by the Walters and Russell Pitts's dad, had collected bits of hearsay about Josh's darkest moments and wanted something to be done. They met with John Prifogle on Monday morning. They said Josh kicked the locker room trash can in the early-season loss to Waldron and called Kurtis Kimla "trash." They were concerned about Josh's profanity in practice, in games, and in the locker room, especially about his use of the word "fuck" (though Josh could not recall an instance when he'd used it) and his predilection for all of the varieties of "Jesus Christ." Toward the end of the hour-and-forty-five-minute meeting with the parents and John Prifogle, the parents were also concerned that he was "too into the game" and "too negative."

The school board members, the superintendent, and John assured Josh that they were not taking the accusations too seriously. For one thing, Alex Layden and Ethan Voss had met with John Prifogle on behalf of the team and had denied all of the accusations, except for Josh being "too into the game." That one confused Alex and Ethan. Josh was, by nature, excitable in game situations. So were most other basketball coaches. Josh was mild-mannered off the court, quiet even. But on the court he fought in his own way for every possession, leaving him drained and sore after every game. *Isn't that what we want in a coach?* Ethan and Alex thought. Their testimony carried enough weight to convince John, the school board, and the superintendent that Josh wasn't doing anything wrong. Everyone around town knew that Ethan and Alex were getting less and less playing time as the season wore on, and now that Logan Alloway was dressing for the varsity team, people expected that Logan might steal minutes from them. They were seniors, and Josh was an outsider who had only been in Milan for two years. If something was wrong—or even if they just didn't like Josh—they would likely be quick to tell someone, especially after allegations were brought up by parents.

But that's not the kind of kids Alex and Ethan were. Truth be told, they loved Josh. Ethan knew that he wasn't performing, and Alex knew basketball was far from his best sport. Alex had even considered quitting basketball before the season started because he knew he would play a limited role and the only junior he got along with was his cousin Braden. Ethan was considered a leader, but the junior class ran the basketball team. All five starters were now juniors, and they had played together since they were grade schoolers. It was intimidating to Ethan and Alex how tight they were because of it. Josh never let the junior class's bond overpower his team, making sure to split guys up at practice. Plus, Ethan and Alex were mature for eighteen-year-olds, and they liked spending time with Josh in his office. Josh felt approachable—one of them.

And Ethan did have one thing to share with John Prifogle. During halftime of the Rising Sun game, Josh did pull Ethan and Braden out of the locker room and told them that they couldn't guard anyone, and if he played them one-on-one, Josh would kick their ass all over the court.

The losing didn't help. It didn't discourage the parents from fibbing—as Josh and the boys swore it was—about Josh's behavior, and it didn't help make the team feel cohesive and committed to winning. It was early February, and Milan had four games left until the tournament. As Tyler put it in the coaches' office, "I'll shit my pants if we go on a run in the tournament. That's what is so great about March."

Any run in the tournament would have to start that weekend against Jac-Cen-Del. Milan would only have to drive ten minutes to the 1A school up the road. Two conference games remained: Jac and Shawe, both 1A schools that they would have no chance of seeing again in the tournament. The wins against Rising Sun and Southwestern Hanover earlier in the year didn't count as conference wins—they were just extra games to fill out the schedule. The designated conference games were all losses for Milan, so the possibility of Milan going winless in the conference was becoming more likely all the time. For one, both Jac and Shawe Memorial were really good teams, and Milan had to play both games away from home. Also, Shawe was ranked in the top ten in 1A all year and had a thousand-point career scorer.

Josh could feel the season start to slip away. He'd tried everything. He tried speeding the game up and relying on his guard-heavy lineup. When Milan did that, they forced shots and turned the ball over. Josh tried slowing the game down, limiting the number of possessions and keeping the game close. When Milan did that, they still forced shots and turned the ball over, and they were unable to defend well enough to make it a good option. Strategically, Josh had exhausted options.

Still, Josh thought that maybe his team could be mentally and emotionally inspired. At Tuesday's practice, he gave each player a sheet of paper and a pen. The paper had a circle in the middle and four blanks for names around the circle. The boys were instructed to write their name in the circle. That was their foxhole. Then they needed to choose four people on the team to be in the foxhole with them.

The results were unsurprising. The Vosses listed each other. The juniors stuck with juniors, and the seniors stuck with seniors. Nearly everyone had John Herzog and Zack Lewis in their foxhole—they were the toughest players on the team. A few of Kurtis's friends listed him, but he was a rare appearance. No one wrote Nick Walter's name down, though that didn't seem to be related to his parents' criticism of Josh. Nick still seemed to believe in Josh and didn't seem to be the source of his parents' information. Everyone knew John Herzog wasn't the source of his dad's information—John barely spoke a word, ever. He was unlikely to complain; it wasn't in his nature.

As Josh completed the scouting report at his desk on Thursday afternoon, he worried about the game against Jac later that night. Jac relied heavily on a player named Trevor Arnett, a six-three forward. As Josh typed "Always DRIVES RIGHT & SPINS BACK LEFT" on the scouting report, he asked Tyler, "How many times do you think we'll let Arnett spin left tonight?" At the end of the report, Josh had a lot of room left on the second page. He was thinking that maybe the scouting reports had been too thorough, that he had given his team too much to think about. So, in big capital letters where detailed offensive and defensive game plans usually went, he wrote: "ME LOSE, WE WIN." Milan's only chance to right the season would rely on the team's cohesion. They hadn't done very well as a collection of individuals thus far.

Josh imagined what the scouting report for Milan might look like. They'd be a fun team to play against, a group of players who all had big gaps in their game. On Wednesday nights, when the Milan Youth Basketball League convened, it didn't look like things would get better soon. Perhaps there are just places where something remarkable only happens once. Perhaps Milan used up all its luck in the fifties. Perhaps time had passed Milan by: whatever it was that made Milan remarkable back then just couldn't survive now.

Josh wasn't concerned with what Milan wasn't. Just hours before their last good chance for a conference win, he was concerned with what they were. He wanted to make sure Milan focused on that—not the controversy swirling around the team, not the pressure of records and conference wins and parents and of students in their classes poking fun at the history. That was one of the things that surprised Ethan about being a Milan basketball player. When he was a kid—and as a kid, he devoured Milan history and watched *Hoosiers* monthly—he thought Milan basketball players must be the popular kids. Must be the focus of the school and town. There was a museum downtown and a major motion picture about the team. But high school had brought the unexpected:

students didn't really care about the basketball team because it seemed so old. Football was in, and winning.

"No one but the people in this room are going to change what's happening," Josh said at the end of the meeting, as the boys rose for their "state" cheer, which had devolved into a whisper of its former volume with every loss. "Me, the coaches, you guys. No one else." It was not only a statement meant to bond the team, it was a dig at whoever was spreading that false information to parents. Or, more likely, it was a dig at their parents, a plea for the boys to become men and tell the adults to butt out of their game.

The Jac-Cen-Del gym had the charm of a grandmother's living room. Everything in the gym seemed to be either bright red or sky blue, the school's unique colors. Photos of past athletic teams hung around the gym, along with banners celebrating conference and sectional championships. An old red curtain was drawn on one end of the gym, hiding the stage the drama club used for their productions. All of the deep red and sky blue gave a strange hue to the gym when the old lights hit everything, making it a little darker than most gyms. As Josh sat on the bench in his warm-ups looking at the banners and pictures—haphazard but many, and Josh would take haphazard and many over two orderly, torn old banners—Jac's coach, David Bradshaw, walked up. His ex-wife was the Milan girls' coach, and she hadn't won a game all year. Bradshaw had won state with Jac two years prior.

"Get you a pop, Josh?" David asked. It was tradition for the home coaches to welcome the visiting coaches with a drink from the concessions stand.

"Diet Mountain Dew, if you have it," Josh said. When David returned with the drink, they talked about fishing. It was a topic that had crept into Josh's conversations more and more lately. With each loss, it seemed Josh sent away for a new bass lure. He and Jill had just planned a trip to Alabama to fish over spring break.

Before the JV game, Nick Walter, Ethan, Braden, and John Herzog sat on the bench, watching the JV guys warm up. Josh was coming from the locker room, and as he walked by, he patted each of them on the head: first Nick, then Ethan, then Braden, then John. Four boys whose parents had caused Josh different and not insignificant amounts of grief over the past couple of weeks. John faked a punch to Josh's midsection and grinned. Josh smiled too as he walked on, no one saying a word. The kids were still with him.

During a time-out in the JV game, as Josh sat alone, watching the game and working on a piece of gum, Kurtis led Nick Ryan, John, and Zack over to sit with Josh.

"What are you doing?" Josh asked. "Go sit over there."

Kurtis smiled, then turned and waved the rest of the team over. Josh rolled his eyes. As Kurtis moved up a row to sit right next to Josh, Josh smiled bigger than he had smiled all month. Jill came into the gym a few minutes later and stopped as she walked in, not believing what she saw. What she had heard about, worried about, for the past two weeks seemed far off as Josh sat surrounded by his players, goofing off. When Jill joined her husband, Kurtis slid over next to her, put his arm around her, and acted like he was flirting with her.

The scene caused Josh to go a little easy on the boys in the locker room before the game. The boys were wrestling around and seemed loose. Josh looked at Jeff and Tyler and jokingly started testing lockers and trash cans out with his toe, in case he needed to kick them over later. The boys loved being a part of this team, and it seemed the boys loved Josh. The team hadn't been this loose all season, for the most part. Why not see if that worked?

It didn't. On the second play of the game, Trevor Arnett drove right, spun back left, and made an easy layup. Milan was down twelve at halftime and sixteen at the end of the third quarter, eventually losing by nineteen. Kurtis's earlier ease with Josh turned into scared looks directed at the bench every time he committed a turnover. Even John's looser-than-usual attitude, fake-punching Josh when he walked by before the game, turned into timidity with the ball. With forty seconds left in the game, Josh called time-out and said, "There's an awful lot of shots in the paint for them. Not a lot for us."

After the game, Josh followed his team to the locker room and stopped before entering. He rested his butt against the door and leaned over so that his body was at a 90-degree angle. It was a position he had been taking more often after games lately. It looked like the stance of someone who just wanted to scream into the floor. Josh was silent, though. Short of inventing new rules, he had no idea how to get this team to win. "What do I say?" Josh asked through his hands, side by side, covering his face. He didn't intend for Jeff or Tyler to answer. Josh pointed the men into the locker room and followed.

"I love you guys," Josh said as he walked into the locker room. In the movie *Hoosiers*, Gene Hackman's character tells the team that he loves them as they're about to beat South Bend Central for the state title. The Hickory team was performing at their highest level, and they had a great deal of confidence. It took time and trust to build that confidence—both Coach Dale's in the boys and the boys' in Coach Dale. Winning helped tremendously. The support of the town's best player didn't hurt either; in fact, it saved Dale's job at the beginning of the movie. Josh believed he had that trust from his boys, but it was a hard type of trust to understand. If he had it, he was lucky to have it. Milan was 4–13. They had lost every conference game so far, and they had just one left against a state-ranked opponent, Shawe Memorial. They had tried playing fast; they had tried playing slow. They tried zone, they tried man-to-man. Nothing worked. Basketball season in Milan had become losing season. That's all winter meant anymore. Milan's recent history was so bad that it seemed unfair to hold basketball season during winter. The ice and the early darkness and the slush and the wind seemed like overkill. Things were bad enough in Milan: they expected a lot and often came close, but always seemed to lose. Why add the gray and cold in too?

Josh walked out of the locker room and found Jill, still sitting in her seat across from the bench. He looked at her and pursed his lips, asking for a kiss. As he bent over and covered his face with his hands, Jeff Stutler played with his granddaughter Emma. John Prifogle carried his young daughter to midcourt and motioned for Josh to come talk to him. Jeff, seemingly knowing what the conversation would be about, ushered his granddaughter back to his daughter and joined them. The conversation was short because Josh walked away.

"That's stupid," Josh said as he walked toward the locker room. "That's ignorant."

"That's why I'm going to take care of it, Josh," John said.

Josh stormed off the court, thinking about Nick Walter's mom claiming that he had said "God damn you" to her oldest son, Alex, during a game Josh's first year at Milan. That was the new evidence they had for John, to show why Josh should be fired.

After Josh had convinced himself that John would in fact take care of it, he took John's daughter from his hands. Jill took this as a sign that it was safe for her to join the men, and she tickled the girl's feet. The Prifogles and the Blankinships walked out of the gym together, but instead of handing the girl back to John, Josh took her on the bus. He had been a little hard on the boys in the locker room. He knew they were trying; he was just frustrated. The postgame moments in the locker room showed him that they were frustrated too. Isn't that what the parents were really complaining about? Frustration? Frustration that the game they spent so much time watching wasn't going according to plan. Frustration that the dreams they had for their boys—bringing a state title back to tiny, old Milan—were looking silly every time they bounced an orange ball on a wood court. Frustration that once the game was over, and they went home defeated, they went home to a place that was worth significantly less than it was a few years ago—a place with fewer jobs that was being left behind in technological access. It was easy to become frustrated about basketball or, on an even smaller scale, the profanities a basketball coach may or may not have uttered. And so they did.

For two minutes, Jill stood in the parking lot, in front of the doorway to the bus. Josh would make a good father someday, she hoped. She watched him take the little girl's arm and wave it at the boys. The boys were unhappy and frustrated, but for a minute Josh made them forget those feelings. For a moment, the boys wanted to be on that bus. Jill thought that would make Josh a good father. Freeing the boys of their frustration, even momentarily, made him a good person. It perhaps even made him a good coach.

14

HYSTERIA

Desperation: 4–13

The youth movement was on in Milan, both on the court and in the locker room. As the varsity team sat in the foul-smelling locker room (later the coaches would discover that one of the shower drains was clogged and holding stale water mixed with Axe shower gel and shampoo), freshman Logan Alloway was showing why he was the future of Milan basketball. Logan was in the middle of one of his nights—nights like the one in late January when he scored thirty-three points against Switzerland County where he was scoring from all over the court. Long three-pointers, dribble drives—it didn't matter to Logan. It didn't matter that he hadn't grown an inch all year, that he was the same five-feet-eight as when he started his freshman year. Logan had found ways to score all year—leaning back a bit on his jump shots, using his body to clear some space on layups and almost giving them a hook shot feel, releasing the ball faster and faster. Sure, he had been doing all of this on the JV level—he started to dress for the varsity team during the Ripley County Tournament at the beginning of January, but he wasn't playing more than a few minutes a game—but he was doing it against guys he had played against since he was a little kid. Ripley County—and neighboring Dearborn, Decatur, Jefferson, Ohio, and Switzerland Counties, for that matter—were small enough that all the kids in the area played together at the only places available, either the Dearborn County Community Center or the Southeastern Indiana YMCA in Batesville.

In the locker room, the youth movement was much younger. Chris Day, an assistant football coach at Milan, had brought his Boys and Girls Club team of seven-year-olds into the locker room to hear the pregame speech. The closest place for kids that young to play organized basketball was in Madison, a forty-five-minute drive south to the Ohio River. Josh's youth basketball league in Milan only accepted players in grades three through six. So Coach Day took a team of Milan kids down to play in Madison—against some future conference opponents at Shawe and Southwestern Hanover, surely—once a week. If their games were decided on nervous energy, the team of Milan kids would have been undefeated. The kids sat on the locker room bleachers, across the room from the varsity team, all bouncing their knees or tapping their feet on the poured concrete floor, which they could just barely reach.

Josh ignored the kids. He had to. Milan hadn't managed a win over the past six games, and the pressure around town (more specifically, in the parents' section) was starting to get to him. It had been a month and four days since Milan beat Rising Sun, thanks to Braden Voss's eight-for-nine three-pointer performance to celebrate his first career start. Some parents were staying after games to talk on the floor, each with their own armchair opinions of what should be changed—tactics, lineups, Josh's attitude.

If they—the boys, the parents, the town, Josh, the other coaches—were counting on a win, it had better come against Scottsburg. After Scottsburg, Milan had two games left before the tournament. The easier of the two on paper was against conference foe Shawe Memorial, the number seven team in Class 1A at the time. In their small, crowded, and loud gym. On their senior night. Their retiring legendary coach's last home game. The other was against Union County, a team who with three players six-feet-five or taller and whose five losses had come at the hands of some of the state's best teams. Scottsburg and their 3–15 record looked like Milan's last shot at a regular-season win.

Josh calmly started his speech. Maybe he wasn't totally ignoring the kids in their Boys and Girls Club T-shirt jerseys.

"I think sometimes you guys worry too much about what I think," he said, sitting on the locker room bench next to Kurtis Kimla. After all, that idea was probably aimed at him more than anyone—no one's body language changed after a postgame speech like Kurtis's. "Don't play tight. Just go play. Get back to thinking you can play with people."

Kurtis didn't know where to look, so he stiffened his back and stared at the ground while keeping his head level, almost looking like he was asleep.

"Think about the teams in our section," Josh said. *North Decatur, South Ripley, Southwestern Hanover, Hauser, Switzerland County.* "We can beat them if we start executing now. Think of this as a sectional-type situation. Scottsburg doesn't know your plays. I know, because they called three teams and asked for tape on us and never picked it up. What does that tell you?"

Scottsburg wasn't taking Milan very seriously, for reasons unknown. The Scottsburg coach hadn't bothered to bring basketballs to Milan and had to ask Josh to borrow a few for warm-up. Then, of course, there was the lack of game preparation that Milan knew about. You could hardly blame Scottsburg, of course. They were 3–15, playing a team they weren't going to see in the postseason since they were in different classes; there was no regional rivalry, and it wasn't a conference game. The game didn't matter much.

But no one had told Josh Blankinship that this game didn't matter. His calm demeanor at the beginning of his talk had picked up in intensity, and his ear was obviously bothering him due to the amount of cotton he was stuffing into it during the talk.

"I would much rather get this done early, you guys go home, eat pizza, hang out with your girlfriends," he said, pacing. "Rather than me sit in my office wondering what we're going to have to do to get a win."

Josh paused in front of the word "win." It was a time he normally would have emphasized that word with a "freaking" or, in rare cases, something stronger. But the Boys and Girls Club team had caught his eye.

"You go execute in front of these kids and whoever else is out there. I'm tired. You guys are tired."

Josh raised his hands to get the guys in a huddle and send them on their way.

"If you're not tired, you're not a competitor," he said.

After the team left, Josh walked over to the group of seven-year-olds. He gathered them all on one bench, all eight of them fitting in the space that Nick Ryan, Nick Walter, and John Herzog had just occupied. Josh looked at Coach Day and gave him a wink.

"Seven and one, coach? Seven and one!" Josh looked at the kids, delivering the speech with the same intensity he would bring to a halftime speech to the varsity team. "That's fantastic. We have to make sure we do things the right way, though. We do that by keeping you in the gym getting better." A little blond boy on the end of the bench twirled his gum around his right index finger. "If you get better as an individual, your team gets better. I'm really proud of you guys. Let's get in here and do a cheer. Indians on three, guys!"

Out in the gym, Jill Blankinship had arrived at the game just a minute before tip-off. She had been sitting in the set of bleachers nearest the door, mostly because she often got off her shift at Major Hospital in Shelbyville just in time to make the games in Milan, about an hour from where she worked. Choosing a seat had become a more involved decision lately, though. Her normal seat was within earshot of the Walters, and they were becoming more vocal about their distaste for her husband's coaching style, specifically the way he motivated players. They thought he was taking things a bit too seriously, heaping too much pressure on the boys. Of course, sitting behind the bench could be worse; that would allow her to hear John Herzog's dad loudly questioning every tactical decision. She opted for her normal seat, near John Prifogle's wife and kids.

If Jill wasn't brave enough to sit behind the bench, John Herzog's dad's territory, the kids from the Boys and Girls Club team had bravery in spades. Or maybe they didn't know any better. Or maybe Josh was just crazy like a fox in that way—a gaggle of seven- and eight-year-olds right behind the bench might temper his enthusiasm on this night. As the team left the court from their warm-up, Nick Ryan took the opportunity to be the type of hometown hero seen in the movies—he flipped a ball to an overly lanky member of the Boys and Girls Club team as he left the court. The boy showed the ball off to his teammates as though it was a foul ball caught in a Major League Baseball game. It looked like something out of a commercial.

There was a noticeable stir in the Milan team as "The Star-Spangled Banner," sung by head cheerleader Stephanie Kirk, ended. A few more chest bumps than usual, a bit more urgency. Scottsburg had treated this game—in their preparations or lack thereof—as an exhibition match. The Milan Indians knew this was their last, best chance for a regular-season win, and on their home court. They hadn't won in front of their fans all year, a woeful 0–6 on their home floor. The painting at midcourt of the Milan floor read "The Heart of Hoosier Hysteria" with a star in the southeastern part of Indiana. All season, it had just been the heartbreak of Hoosier Hysteria.

Tyler Theising leaned into Josh's ear. "They're fired up tonight," he said, smiling, surprised.

"Hell, they oughta be." Josh said, looking back at the full Milan student section.

Late in the game on offense, it seemed as if the only option was John Herzog. He had beaten his defender all night, and two minutes into the fourth quarter, Milan was down only four points. Zack Lewis was in foul trouble, which caused John Herzog to handle the ball more—something his father had been advocating for from his spot in the bleachers.

Josh looked at his bench. "Zack, get Nick Walter," he said, wanting Zack Lewis on the court for, at the very least, his good on-the-ball defense.

"Leave it alone!" Ed Herzog yelled. "Leave the lineup alone!" Milan was finally closing the gap, and doing it with John Herzog at the point. Ed didn't want to see that messed up. On the next Milan possession, Kurtis bobbled a pass from John, and Scottsburg stole the ball. Even though Josh's substitution had nothing to do with the play, Ed Herzog stood and yelled again. "Leave the lineup alone!"

But Milan kept chipping away, thanks to Ed's son. With four minutes left, John drove to the basket and scored on a reverse layup to tie the score at 48–48. The game tightened up at that point, and with a minute and a half left, Josh called a time-out, down 53–52.

"There's a lot of time left," Josh instructed. "Just get the ball in bounds and go from there."

From the moment the ball was inbounded to Zack Lewis, none of the Milan players except for John Herzog looked particularly confident. What followed was a series of hot-potato passes from one nervous Indian to the next. Milan players weaved in and out on the perimeter, handing the ball off to one another, making simple passes, but passes that said *Here, you take it.* After thirty seconds, John Herzog had seen enough. He collected the ball from Braden Voss at the top of the key and drove past three Scottsburg defenders, casually tossing the ball off the backboard and in. Milan had a one-point lead with forty-two seconds left. Did they go for a shot too early? Should they have worn the clock down until the last shot? Scottsburg took a time-out.

"You have to play the best forty-two seconds of defense of your life!" Josh screamed, losing his voice. His voice was starting to crack and become weak, a high-pitched shriek at the ends of his sentences. "You think one thing when their shot goes up—block out. They have to foul when they miss."

It wasn't Scottsburg that was going to do the fouling. With thirty seconds left, Nick Walter—who was in because Nick Ryan had fouled out—got caught up in a screen and allowed Scottsburg to enter the ball to Brad Bowling on the right block. Nick Walter sprinted over and hacked Bowling right as he shot. The ball bounced off the backboard, off the rim, and out. But Scottsburg's best player had two foul shots, and he made both of them to reclaim a one-point lead for Scottsburg.

Zack Lewis brought the ball up and passed to John Herzog on the right wing. And, just as he had done all game, Herzog dribbled past his defender. But Scottsburg was ready for it. Two defenders rotated over and cut John off from the basket, forcing him underneath. Herzog had no choice but to jump—he was about to run out of bounds. Suddenly, he saw a flash from the left wing. Braden Voss, a player who rarely seemed at home inside the three-point line, instinctively cut toward the basket. Just as John Herzog's foot was about to come down out of bounds, he whipped the ball to Braden, who was wide open for a layup. Milan had a one-point lead with ten seconds left. Josh, nervously watching from midcourt as Scottsburg bungled their last possession, galloped down the sideline and pumped his fist, narrowly missing a Milan cheerleader. Braden and Ethan Voss hugged at midcourt, Braden almost crying. Braden had the winning shot and steal, and played a big role in his brother's getting at least one home win in his senior season.

In the locker room, the boys were rowdy. It had been over a month since they won a game, and they spent a few minutes going over every successful play. As Josh walked into the locker room, Zack Lewis stood up and shouted, "I can tell you this, we're not practicing tomorrow!"

Josh looked at him and smiled. "Oh yes, we are," he said. Josh took a minute to collect himself. His voice was weak, and he looked totally out of energy. Josh knelt, bent at the knees in a squat position, touching the floor with his right hand. He sighed, trying to catch his breath. He looked like he was about to throw up. He didn't have the energy to match the boys' enthusiasm. Plus, what was there to say after a game like that? "That," Josh started, "that was one hell of a comeback after the atrocious third quarter we had."

The boys couldn't wait to get out on the court to their friends and family. They took two-minute showers—rinses, really—and hugged their parents, laughing about the win they finally managed.

Especially after a win, it would have been normal for Josh to hang out in his office with Coach Stutler and Coach Theising, breaking down film until one or two in the morning. Jill Blankinship knew it might take a bit longer tonight, though, because Josh had another person to catch up with—Todd Satterly, one of the officials from the night's game. Todd was the girls' basketball coach at New Albany High School, a friend and colleague of Josh's when Josh taught there just two years ago. Thirty minutes after the game, Jill walked down the tunnel behind the home bleachers, past the locker room and the coaches' office, and knocked on the referees' locker room. She didn't wait to hear "come in" after she knocked, but walked right in to see Josh sitting on a teacher's desk in the office, talking to Todd as he got dressed after his postgame shower. "Jesus, Jill, I'm in my shorts here," Todd said, looking up at her in the doorway. "Aw, I'm a nurse," Jill said. She waited for him to put on his pants and walked over and gave him a hug. "How are you, Todd?"

Todd said that he was fine. "How are you two, doing, though?" Todd had already heard from Josh about everything basketball-related—how he had trouble with parents (nothing new for any coach, Todd noted), how he had hoped they'd be much better than last year but only had two more wins this year than last, how they just kept finding ways to lose at the end of close games. The question wasn't about the basketball season. The question was about what was happening in every school around the state of Indiana.

Three weeks earlier, the Indiana Senate labor committee had advanced a proposal, by a vote of 7–2, to strip Indiana teachers of collective bargaining rights. Moves like this were happening all over the country, most notably in Wisconsin, but were gaining little media coverage in Indiana. Teachers around the state were counting it as just one more step limiting their ability to find jobs, keep jobs, and be paid a fair wage.

Things were more serious in Milan than they were in many parts of the state. Milan had made headlines in the *Indianapolis Star* in January, when the interim superintendent, Steve Gookins, proposed taking away coaching stipends and making all coaching positions in the school corporation volunteer-only. Milan needed to cut $368,000 from their budget, and Gookins estimated that taking all coaching stipends away would save $210,000.

"Well, you know they cut my pay in half last year, don't you, Todd?" Josh said. When Josh was hired the year before, he signed a two-year contract with the school system. He was paid $6,000 as a coaching stipend on top of his salary as a physical education teacher. In the 2010–11 school year, Gookins cut all coaching stipends in half and eliminated some coaching positions altogether. Josh lost a coaching position in the process, leaving Milan with a varsity head coach, a junior varsity head coach, and a freshman coach. No program assistant, and less pay for the same job.

During the season, Josh often arrived at school at 6 a.m. to let Jake White shoot before school, and left around 8 p.m. On game days, Josh could cross the threshold of his house as late as 2:30 a.m. After practices, he often drove to meet coaches from other schools in the parking lot of a McDonald's or at a gas station to exchange game tape. Or if an upcoming opponent was playing during an off-night for Milan, Josh would drive to scout the opposing team. All that extra time, all that gas—hovering around $3.50 a gallon—and less pay. Add that to the time Josh spent taking the team to summer camps and supervising summer workouts, and the pay cut felt like a personal attack.

"Shoot, I hadn't heard that, Josh," Todd said, putting his shoes on. "What's going on? Isn't this Milan? *Hoosiers* and all that?" Josh shook his head. The article in the *Star* three weeks ago had left him feeling like it didn't matter that Milan was constantly pointed to in the state and beyond as an inspiration, that it didn't matter where you came from, or how big you were, or how big the odds were, that you could achieve something through hard work. "As bad as [this situation] is, [maybe it] is a chance to step back and re-evaluate what direction we're headed," Gookins was quoted as saying. He singled out basketball, even. "Why do we need to play organized basketball 12 months of the year?" Gookins asked. "The coaches get burned out. But they say we have to do it because everyone else is. Maybe if we go to volunteer coaching, we'll get it back to where it needs to be."

"You know," Josh said, "I got RIFed last year." Josh shook his head. The head coach of the Milan Indians. Any head basketball coach in Indiana. Pink-slipped.

Reduction in force notices, or RIFs, were becoming common in Indiana. In late 2009, Governor Mitch Daniels announced that school districts around the state would receive $300 million less than they originally expected over the next eighteen months. Eleven days after his initial announcement, on December 29, 2009, Daniels announced that the cuts would happen over the next year—not over eighteen months. Schools started advising teachers through RIF notices that they were being laid off—even those with contracts. Some, everyone knew, would be hired back. But it was rare for a school to be able to hire every teacher back.

RIF notices were based strictly on seniority within departments. If the superintendent and the school board decided that it looked like they would have to fire two elementary school teachers, the two newest teachers were RIFed. It didn't matter if those teachers were the best ones at the school; they were let go. Of course, Josh had only been at Milan for a year. The day after the 2009–10 season ended with a sectional loss against Hauser, Josh had a RIF notice in his mailbox. It was hard not to find the timing coincidental, although it had nothing to do with the team's 3–17 final record in his first year as coach.

"So, it gets down to the last day that people can declare for retirement or switch departments," Josh said, smiling. "And I looked screwed. But Ryan

Langferman, our football coach, was wanting to switch to science from physical education, so we had a little hope. But it didn't look like a science job was going to open up for him, so it looked like he was going to get the last PE spot, and I'd be out of a job, Milan would be out of a head coach, everything. So I'm making copies, and this science teacher walks up to me and says, 'I understand that if a science job opens up, you get to stay.' I said, 'Yes, that's right.'" Josh grinned. "Todd, I shit you not, he handed me his letter of resignation and said, 'Well, enjoy it.'"

Todd couldn't understand the situation. "I don't get it, Josh. Milan was really going to go without a head basketball coach? Couldn't they cut anything else?"

Without a doubt, Josh told Todd, Milan could cut something else. Despite having only four hundred students, Milan hosted every Indiana High School Athletic Association sport besides gymnastics. Nineteen sports for four hundred students. Milan didn't have a pool, but they had a swim team with six members. Their soccer team was coed. And every one of those nineteen sports took up coaching stipend money, many of them with paid assistants. Milan's focus was no longer on basketball.

The next morning before practice, Josh looked at the broken ceiling tile sitting on his desk. He signed it, "John, sorry. Milan–56, Scottsburg–55. Halftime. Go Indians! Josh" and put it on John Prifogle's desk. "He'll get a kick out of that," Josh told Stutler.

At the beginning of practice, Josh went through his normal day-after-a-game routine of talking to the boys about the game, discussing the stats, talking about what they needed to do to improve. The scoreboard had been left on overnight, and 56–55 still showed.

As the boys shot around, going through a lighter workout, since everyone was still tired from the game the night before, Josh walked around the court, kicking up the sealant that was cracking all over the floor. He gathered a bunch of clear plastic chips in his hand.

"I don't like the white in the background of 'Hoosier Hysteria,'" Josh said to Coach Stutler and Coach Theising, pointing to the painting at center court.

Theising chuckled. "I don't like having Hoosier Hysteria on the court, period," he said.

Stutler looked at Theising in disbelief. He knew Theising could never understand. Tyler was just a kid from the county over, and young. He didn't know—couldn't know, not like Jeff Stutler knew—what "Hoosier Hysteria" meant.

"It's Milan, Tyler," Jeff said, shaking his head.

"Livin' in the past," Tyler said.

Stutler couldn't take it. "Livin' in the past?" he asked, voice raised in a manner unusual for the normally soft-spoken Milan alumnus. "You are a communist! Milan did more for Indiana basketball than any other team." Jeff shook his head. "Hell, I've seen people come from New Zealand to take pictures of this floor."

Josh shrugged at Tyler as if to say, *You know, he's right.* And then Josh walked over to a trash can in the corner of the gym and threw the chipped pieces of the deteriorating gym floor away.

15

THE MILAN EVERYONE EXPECTS

February 22: 5–13

Milan was set to play Shawe on Jill's birthday, so she joined Josh at Ison's Family Pizza in Batesville the night before. She was looking forward to the evening: Josh was taking her to Bonefish Grill in Cincinnati. She wore a black sweater with dark jeans and put on a bit more makeup than usual.

Before her birthday dinner, she had to go with Josh to Ison's. Every Monday night, Ron Raver, a retired high school coach, would drive his motorized scooter up the ramp at Ison's, head to the back room, and set up his radio equipment. He hosted a radio show, *Coaches Corner*, that aired from 6 to 7 p.m. on WRBI out of Batesville. Each week he would have a coach from one of the Ripley County schools on to discuss area high school athletics. Each week he would invite people to come on down to Ison's and listen to the show in the stark, unadorned back room. Each week the audience was mostly coaches' wives.

The show on February 21 was Ron's favorite of the year. Each year, for the show after the sectional draw, Ron had the four Ripley County coaches on the show. They discussed their draw and gave fans a recap of their season to that point, and Ron usually talked with the coaches about the keys to their sectionals. Despite his age and poor health, Coach Raver (as the guests called him) managed to see many area basketball games. He had coached basketball at Batesville High School for nineteen years, where he had also coached cross country for thirty years and track for forty-seven years. He coached varsity basketball for three years and had a 46–19 record. (Milan lost seventeen games in Josh's first year.)

The first thing Josh did when he walked into Ison's was talk to David Bradshaw, who was there wearing his Jac-Cen-Del jogging suit. Milan had drawn Hauser High School in the first round, a team they played early in the season. Jac had played them a couple of weeks before the show, and Josh wanted to know if their style of play had changed much. Jill sat down at a plastic-topped table on a metal folding chair in the back room of Ison's while Josh asked David if they were still playing their big kids a lot and if Silas Sims was shooting the ball any better. While Jill checked her phone for text messages, David mapped a play out for Josh on his hand, using his index finger as the ball.

"They'll want a track meet, Josh," David said when he showed him the play.

"Do you think we need to slow it down? I think that killed us against you," Josh said. David waffled on answering that question. He wanted Josh to succeed—it didn't matter to him now if Milan excelled, really. If anything, David would love for Milan to beat Shawe the next night because Shawe and Jac-Cen-Del were in the same 1A section. Still, David didn't know what it would take for Milan to start winning. Milan was looking worse as the season went on, not better. David saw it in the game tapes. Beating Scottsburg wouldn't change that.

Ron interrupted David and Josh right when David was going to be forced to answer Josh's question.

"Guys, we'll be just a second. Having trouble with the remote connection," Ron said.

Josh took his turn first with Coach Raver. After the win against Scottsburg, Josh said, he hoped things were headed in the right direction.

"So, what do you have left, Coach?" Ron asked.

Josh chuckled. "Nothing too easy." Shawe was still ranked in the top ten, and Union County had a 13–5 record against better opponents than Milan had played. Josh was looking forward to Union County, since they were basically a better Hauser—tall and athletic. Union County started three players taller than Nick Ryan and brought a six-foot-seven kid off the bench. Josh let his mind slip to his team for a moment while he was on the radio. *How did every other school Milan's size get big kids?*

The conversation turned to Braden Voss. Lately, Braden was establishing himself as the second most productive scorer on the team.

"He's sure not very physical, is he Josh?" Ron asked, wiping a bead of sweat off his liver-spotted forehead.

Josh talked about the need for Braden to be less one-dimensional. When Braden takes the ball to the rim, he's not bad, Josh explained. He needs to do that more to keep people from guarding him so close. Again, the conversation turned to size. It'd be nice, Josh explained, for them to have the size of Batesville, Jac-Cen-Del, and South Ripley, the schools in their county. It would allow Braden more room to work, and it would win them games. Josh mentioned a freshman who was going to dress for sectionals—not by name, but it was Logan Alloway—who was good but, again, under six feet tall.

"Anything else you want to say, Josh?" Ron asked.

Josh closed by thanking the parents for all of their dedication that year. Jill rolled her eyes as Josh smiled at her. On the radio, Josh could be sarcastic and the show's listeners wouldn't know.

But the parents of the boys would know. The day before, Josh had sent the boys home with a letter for their parents. It read:

To the Parents of Milan Basketball:

I hope this letter finds all of you well as we close in on the start of the STATE TOURNAMENT and SECTIONAL 44 at South Ripley High School. I want to take this opportunity to highlight a few items and discuss our 2010–2011 basketball season. First I want to personally thank every parent for organizing the TEAM meals before and after every game. That is a luxury that cannot go without recognition and I once again thank you all for providing our TEAM meals.

Secondly, I want to discuss our season thus far. At the beginning of the season our coaching staff set numerous goals for our players and TEAM. Our first goal was to win our FIRST GAME versus the Lawrenceburg Tigers. Our TEAM accomplished that goal by defeating the Tigers on the ROAD in overtime 52–49. By accomplishing that goal our players did something a Milan Basketball team had not done since November 30th, 2002 . . . Win a SEASON OPENING GAME! Since that time our TEAM has been riding a roller coaster and our overall record is not where we thought it would be at this time. However, our players have continued to improve as people, student-athletes, and being great citizens of the Milan Community.

Furthermore, I think it is important to point out that our TEAM has made tremendous strides in several facets of the game of basketball. Last season our TEAM averaged 17 turnovers per game while only averaging 14.9 this season. Another TEAM stat our program has improved from last season to this season is our overall defensive average (points scored by our opponent). Overall, we have cut 5.9 PPG from last season where we gave up 62.1 PPG while only giving up 56.2 this season, which is the lowest defensive average Milan has had since the 2000–2001 season. These stats among several others have continued to improve because of the dedication your son(s) have shown to our BASKETBALL TEAM and PROGRAM. In addition to those items, our TEAM has had the opportunity to "win" as stated in the MILAN DOZEN, 13 out of the 16 games so far this season. Offensively, we are averaging 51.5 PPG and our opponents are once more averaging 56.2, which means we are getting beat by 4.7 PPG compared to 11.9 last season.

In conclusion, I have been informed that we have several parents upset with me regarding how their son is being treated. I assure you that your son(s) are not being mistreated in any way. Please understand that we have an open door policy and if you would like to set up a meeting to discuss any of these issues please contact Mr. John Prifogle or myself and we would be more than willing to set up a meeting. Our open door policy also includes our team practices for the remainder of the season. I have enclosed a practice schedule for the rest of the season and if you have any questions please contact me. Thank you for your continued support of Milan Basketball!

Once an Indian, Always an Indian!

Josh Blankinship

Milan High School

Varsity Basketball Coach

Josh was comfortable in reinforcing his criticism of the parents with capital letters just as he was comfortable sending a sarcastic message over the radio to the offending group. To Josh, the parents were ungrateful. Milan had been a program in trouble when he arrived a year and a half earlier. One season, they'd had more losses than Coach Raver had in a three-year career. His team was outmuscled and outsized every game, even against schools with half of the enrollment of tiny Milan.

There was a reason the Milan '54 state champs banner was worn and water-damaged. There was a reason the water tower with the same message was dilapidated. It wasn't the boys who cared if they lived up to the Milan name. Sure, they wanted to win. It was frustrating to lose games by fine margins, as they had all season, to lose games because the talent wasn't quite there, not because the effort wasn't. It was the parents who wanted to win because of the place. Because of the name. Because of the past. In the end, it was the legend that damned Milan—the parable that made the nowhere town famous: that it didn't matter how skilled or tall or athletic a basketball team was, that if you were from Milan and you worked hard, you could be unstoppable.

It was the legend that frustrated Ethan, and it was the legend that kept Ethan from voicing his frustration. March was coming. No one wanted to rock the boat because of how the parable ends. Milan wins. David slays Goliath. It was in the book that the Vosses cracked each Sunday in the pews of Milan United Methodist Church. The boys stayed close because they believed. But the parents were upset because they knew that the miracle didn't work like this—teams didn't win state championships with losing records. The parents knew that Milan could win one if only things were perfect. But once they removed Josh, would that really fix things? They knew the problem couldn't be their kids, of that winning Milan stock. It must have been the outsider.

The outsider shook hands with Coach Raver as he went to commercial. "Good luck, Coach," Ron said. It was hard to tell whether he meant with the rest of Milan's games or with the problems he had with the program, which were no secret to insiders like Ron.

Josh smiled at Jill as he walked over to her and put on his jacket, a Butler jacket with the Final Four logo on it, from Butler's run in the NCAA tournament the year before. That run had brought TV cameras from around the nation to Milan. Everyone used Milan as the example that Butler could really win the national championship. Small school, controlled play, outsized but not outsmarted. They won when they shouldn't. Everyone wanted to see the state champs trophy and the banners. But no one commented on Milan's 3–17 record that year. No one noticed that the team that proved Butler could "really do it" hadn't been able to manage a winning season in six years. Milan had the same number of one- or two-win seasons as they did winning seasons. The modern game had passed Milan by. And still the parable was told.

"That felt good," Josh said, referring to his dig at the parents. "Let's go eat." For the night, Josh and Jill would forget about the group of parents threatening Josh's job. And although Josh's job hung in the balance—even though he had received unofficial votes of confidence from the school board and the superintendent and John Prifogle—they would continue to toy with the idea of finally becoming parents themselves.

The letter seemed to have little effect on Brian Voss. He brought the team's dinner—pizza from Batesville—into the school cafeteria at 3:20 p.m. and passed by Josh without saying a word. As he walked past, Josh said, "Thanks, Brian!" Only then did Brian acknowledge Josh. Brian wasn't the main focus of the letter—he was at least open with Josh when he had a problem. In fact, Josh might prefer that Brian grumble behind his back rather than call him on the phone to complain for nearly an hour.

The boys took their pizza into the coaches' office to review the scouting report for Shawe. It was Milan's last chance to win a conference game. Not being able to win a single conference game would mean that they hadn't improved on the previous season, a season that ended with ten straight losses. Last year, people hadn't expected much. This year, Milan had a core group of juniors who led the team. They were older, more experienced. It was time to prove it in the conference.

Josh spent most of the time focused on the motivational quotes at the bottom of the scouting report. A long season was coming to a close, and this was the last meaningful game Milan would play before the tournament. Josh was already talking about the tournament with the coaches and the players, both directly and indirectly. *It's the time of year when anything can happen. It's the time of year when anything does happen.* He had been inserting similar sentiments at the end of his team talks since the loss against Jac-Cen-Del. When the sectional pairings were announced on the radio the previous Sunday night, he and Ethan had exchanged texts. They'd get another shot at Hauser. They hadn't played well against Hauser earlier in the year, but while everyone would expect Hauser to win, Ethan and Josh intended to have their say in the matter.

As Ethan, Braden, and Brian Voss heard the pairing, they leaned back in their seats around the radio and smiled. Hauser was the second-best team in the section, probably. It was a team they knew well, and a team they thought they could beat if things fell their way. Plus, what good would it do for them to think they were defeated? Recent history—recent cultural history included—told them that Milan didn't stand much of a chance against anyone, especially not those big farmboys from Bartholomew County. Ethan's first thought was to text Josh. They could run those lugs out of the gym.

And so the preparation for Shawe wasn't so much about winning a conference game as much as it was preparing for the type of battle they'd encounter in the tournament in a week and a half. Instead of the spacious South Ripley gym, the game against Shawe would take place in the dingy Shawe Memorial gym, which had the yellowish hue of a partly finished basement.

"Let's go to a dump tonight and beat the number nine team in the state," Josh told the boys as he collected them for their "state" cheer.

After the boys left to collect their things in the locker room, Josh told Jeff and Tyler about running into Brian before the meeting. "I took the high road, of course," Josh said. "I'm surprised he showed up." Josh was falling into the habit of telling Jeff and Tyler about his every encounter with the parents. He kept a tone that suggested he thought the parents' actions were funny or pathetic. He would shake his head and smirk when he told Jeff about what his son-in-law was up to, just to show that it was no skin off his back if Brian Voss wanted to complain about Ethan's diminishing role on the team. The stat line had shown that Josh made a productive choice swapping Ethan out for his little brother.

But while Josh kept a light tone when he told Jeff and Tyler about the latest parent drama, the fact that he kept bringing the drama up suggested that he was actually quite worried about his job, his career, the team's cohesion, and his legacy in Milan. Josh had no problem talking to Jeff about Brian, because Josh knew Jeff agreed with him on the Ethan situation—he couldn't play defense very well, and he struggled to shoot well early in the season. Braden was simply a better fit for this team, no matter how many buzzer beaters to win the state championship Ethan sunk on his papaw's court. A win against Shawe on their senior night would do a lot to help the mood. A run in the tournament, though, would be Milan's favored form of redemption. Wins erase memories, but tournament wins recall memories, especially in Milan.

The trip to Shawe started poorly. Logan Alloway was suspended for one and a half quarters in the JV game because he was late to the team meeting after school. Still, when he came into the game, the Shawe JV coach charged up the sideline and yelled at his team, "Number three is in! Number three is in! He's that shooter!" Even at the JV level, teams were not only starting to notice Logan but also to prepare for him.

The boys were crammed into a locker room built for ten students at the end of the gym. It was just inside a small hallway to the side of the stage that sat a couple of yards past the end line at the end of the floor. As the JV players came in following their 49–40 loss, the varsity players could tell by Jeff's unusually unpleasant demeanor that it was their cue to go out and sit on the edge of the stage while they waited for their younger teammates to be yelled at, after which they would receive their final instructions before warm-up. The JV squad had played—and lived, in Logan's case—without discipline. The coaches had seen it all year—a cut class here, a picked fight in practice there—and were tired of it. It was rare that Josh got involved with the JV team, but he had seen enough. Plus, it was the end of the season, and a couple of the JV players were expected to take varsity spots next year. That wouldn't be tolerated at the next level.

Josh was still running hot when the JV team went into the hallway before their showers so that the varsity team could talk. His voice was already cracking, and he could tell that this would be another exhausting night. The older boys were calm and loose, way too laid back for Josh's liking, especially since Shawe was a ranked team and their last conference opponent.

"If you can't get fired up for playing a state-ranked team, then there is no excuse for you," Josh said. The boys started to perk up as they heard the crowd cheer for the Hilltoppers as they took the court for warm-up. "And let me tell you something," Josh said, making sure to look each of the juniors in the eye. "Get used to what it's like to play and beat a state-ranked team. Because when you do that, you start becoming a state-ranked team." Most of the boys feigned excitement as they clapped their hands. Ethan and Braden looked at each other and smiled.

They didn't mind so much that their teammates didn't quite believe the story that Josh was telling them, that Milan could be ranked again. It was fun to believe that they could. It was fun to believe that all those games in the driveway with the red sunset peeking through the browned cornstalks in late August— when their friends were off at football practice—meant something. Prepared them for something. And not just the something of playing for the Milan Indians, that team that once played so well a movie had been made about them. Prepared them for something that they could have a say in. Ethan thought it was fun to believe that they could make a run in the tournament, suddenly get Hollywood-hot and produce their own movie-worthy script. In his mind, he knew it wasn't likely, but for the next week or two weeks or, if things went really well, the next month, he was going to lead with his heart. On the bench, on the court, on the bus, in the locker room. Ethan knew that this was the moment he had been waiting his whole life. Tournament time, senior year, his cousin and his little brother at his side. He wasn't in the mood to take it for granted.

Braden knew all about Ethan's dreams. They were his dreams too. Besides, they had spent way too many late nights playing PlayStation and talking about what it would be like to bring a trophy back to the town that so desperately needed a basketball trophy. The football team's success was nice, but it never seemed enough for those visitors from out of town who stopped by the school to see the banner and the trophy from 1954. "How's the team doing now?" the tourists would ask, expecting the best for Milan because they had never been told any different. The football team's record would never satisfy them.

"All that Xs and Os stuff don't matter," Josh told the team as they got into their huddle, Ethan's hand on Braden's, and Braden's hand on Alex's, and Alex's hand on Josh's. The Voss boys knew that for sure.

What did matter to the people in the gym was Jerry Bomholt, Shawe's coach for the past thirty-one years. He was retiring from coaching at the end of the season. Shawe had ninety-three students, and every one of them seemed to be in their 826-seat gym. They were as loud as any big-school gym after Coach Bomholt said his good-byes.

In a way, Shawe represented the things that people thought Milan stood for. They were a small school like Hickory, only ninety-three students. Milan was nearly four times the size of Shawe. And yes, Shawe was a private Catholic school, so they could be selective about their students, make sure that they had the requisite athletes to fill out each of their sports teams. But it was hard not to think of Hickory—and to think of Hickory is to think of Milan—when the capacity crowd of over eight times the school's enrollment rose to their feet to thank the departing coach. Bomholt had built a winner at a small school, and they were expected to challenge for the state title that year.

That's what people expected when they thought about Milan: a small school defying the odds and finding ways to win against all evidence as to why they shouldn't. People expected a magic in the air. Perhaps that's why the people who spread the Milan gospel ignored the present: it didn't make sense that Milan wasn't producing winners and hadn't for some time. It didn't match up with the story of 1954, and it didn't match up with the story told in *Hoosiers*. Hard work and want-to was supposed to get a team somewhere.

Milan played with plenty of emotion, but on that particular night the want-to hurt them in the end.

Zack Lewis came out of the game midway through the third quarter, and John Herzog moved to point guard, a position his father thought best suited him. But that's when things fell apart for Milan. Shawe went on a 15–2 run to close the third quarter, capped by Josh getting a technical foul for criticizing the refereeing. The game became ugly, and Josh thought the referees weren't helping matters—John was undercut as he jumped to take a shot, but the referees called him for traveling. He fouled out with four minutes left in the game, and

Kurtis followed close behind. When Kurtis came out of the game, he was still mad, despite the large deficit.

"That's bullshit," Kurtis said as he passed Josh. As he walked to the end of the bench, Josh followed him.

"Is that the way you want it to be?" Josh asked. "I don't care if it's right or wrong, you keep your mouth shut."

Zack Lewis had been frustrated by the aggressive on-the-ball defense of Shawe all night. Zack often was the first of the Milan players to start jawing with the other team, and he had started early with Shawe's star, Joey Mingione. The game really started to simmer, though, when Milan decided to let Shawe hold the ball in the last two minutes. Milan was down seventeen points, and they decided not to foul to extend the game. Shawe tossed the ball to Joey Mingione in the backcourt, and Zack Lewis pushed Mingione in the face, earning a flagrant foul. Josh quickly pulled him out of the game.

"I get you're frustrated," Josh said, kneeling in front of Zack. "I get that. But there's no reason for that."

The mood was somber in the hallway outside the locker room, as it had been so many times before. Milan had stayed with a very good team for about two and a half quarters and ended up losing by nineteen points. Milan was tough, but only for twenty minutes. One thing had gone wrong, and it snowballed, picking up technical fouls and flagrant fouls and cold shooting along the way. As the coaches headed into the locker room, Tyler told Josh with an odd sense of calm, "You're away, and things happen on the road." He stated it as fact, as if it were silly to dream that Milan wouldn't face the kind of adversity they faced that night. The way things were happening to Milan, he could have simply said, "You're Milan, and things happen to Milan."

Josh stayed positive in the locker room despite the winless conference mark. "Refocus and be done with it, because I'm done with it," Josh said. "That was a really good team we played with for a half." March was coming, and it wasn't a time to dwell on anything that could make the boys question whether or not they could make a run in the tournament.

Later, on the bus, the boys found a way to get some positives out of the night. Zack turned to Ben Lawhorn and told the tale of his flagrant foul. "I swung, like *that,* and I heard someone flop and I was like *oh, shit.*"

Alex Layden turned around. "Didn't he have braces? If you would have connected, you would have cut him wide open!"

In the front of the bus, Josh held the stat book from the night in one hand and dumped Cheetos straight from the bag into his mouth with the other. The only player who scored in double figures was Ethan, who had eighteen points. His little brother hadn't produced the way he normally did, and John was held scoreless. If Ethan could score a little, Milan could win, but only with normal output from Braden and John. Josh felt like every time he plugged a hole in the leaking bucket of Milan basketball, another leak sprang. Josh was sure he'd hear from Brian about his son's good night.

Josh put the stat book away. The night's events had made his ear intolerable, and he retrieved some eardrops from his jacket pocket. As he tipped his head into the aisle of the bus, he caught Jeff's attention. Josh motioned back to Zack Lewis as the boy finished up his exaggerated story. "How stupid is he?" Josh asked, shaking his head. "He could have gotten kicked out for that one."

After Jeff didn't answer, Josh pushed further. "Who's even going to be our backup point guard next year?" The results when Zack came out of the game that night weren't good. They promised to be worse next year.

Jeff had no answers, so he started a conversation about how much they dreaded teaching the next morning. Jeff was teaching his eighth-graders about the War of 1812. He yawned and looked out the window as the night pushed 11 p.m. because of the retirement ceremony. "I'm so tired, I'll just probably have them watch a DVD."

But Josh removed himself from the conversation, leaving Jeff mainly talking to Tyler. Josh picked up the stat book again and looked at it, hoping the third-quarter numbers would change. He tossed it back on his bag and turned around to look at Jeff.

"What does any of that have to do with winning a basketball game?" Josh asked, silencing Tyler and Jeff. Usually Josh would engage in the conversation. But Milan was winless in the conference again, and they only had one game left before the tournament. They needed to get confident, they needed to produce winning basketball, and they needed it ten games ago. Senior night was just three days away, when Josh would say good-bye to Ethan and Alex. Ethan would get his starting position back for one game, and Josh was happy about that. He earned it with his performance against Shawe. If anything, he wouldn't have to worry about Brian calling him and petitioning for Ethan's inclusion.

16

SENIOR NIGHT

February 25: 5–14

The Milan High School senior night booklet was black-and-white, letter-sized sheets of paper, photocopied and folded down the middle and stapled for binding. The front page showed Ethan and Alex in their home whites, with the three senior cheerleaders in front of them, their hands on their hips while Ethan and Alex stood with their arms awkwardly at their sides. Next to that was a picture of one of the cheerleaders and Elaina Voss—Alex and Ethan's cousin—in their Milan girls' basketball uniforms. The girls' team was worse off than the boys' team that year—they hadn't won a game. Below the girls was a picture of the twelve band seniors, and next to them was a picture of the two senior basketball managers, the girls' manager and Jamie Altieri, the boys' manager.

On Ethan's senior night page he included two pictures—one of him as a baby, and one of him in a suit and a crown, with a sash that said "HOMECOMING KING" draped over his shoulder. Ethan wasn't the coolest kid in school. Other students made fun of him for romanticizing Milan basketball and insisting on watching *Hoosiers* on a near-monthly basis. Ethan couldn't help it; he was too earnest to hide his pride in his town and school, as dated as that pride was. It wasn't Ethan's popularity that carried him to Homecoming King status. It was that earnestness.

In the picture, Ethan looked at the camera hopefully, knowing that this would be the season that Milan returned to glory. The new coach had a year under his belt, his brother's promising sophomore class had become juniors, and it was his senior year—the one Ethan played out on his grandfather's hoop so many times as a kid. Ethan, the Ethan in the photo, knew only one script for the story.

As Ethan walked across the court to shake Josh's hand and receive gifts from the moms—a water cooler, pillow, laundry bin, balloons, and a flower—he had a hard time reconciling his dreams with the reality. Milan had finished the conference schedule winless and had managed only five wins all season. Ethan didn't know how to feel about it all. He was proud of those five wins—the first season-opening win for a Milan team in nine years, plus a win that let them play for a tournament championship. Another win was special for other reasons—it had been his little brother's first start, and Braden had torched the Rising Sun Shiners for thirty points. Ethan had scored only six from his new— and by senior night, permanent—role on the bench.

Ethan's mom, Deb, took her son by the arm and forced him into escorting her to center court as his name was read. Brian Voss followed a step behind and more than an arm's length from Ethan and his ex-wife. He made sure to position his ex-wife on Josh's side as they walked up to the coach. Brian seemed zoned out and didn't talk to Josh at all, preferring to let Ethan and Deb do the talking. They moved on to center court with Brian still not saying a word.

Next, Alex Layden walked onto the court with his dad and mom, who was Brian's little sister. After talking to Josh and watching as Alex received his senior night gifts, Anne Marie Layden tried poking her older brother Brian to force a smile out of him. It didn't work.

Josh saved his most sincere attitude for Jamie Altieri and his mother. Josh was happy to have Jamie that season, and Jamie liked being around the team. Josh talked to Vicki Altieri at midcourt while Randy Combs told the crowd over the PA that Jamie planned to attend Ohio Technical Institute for a motorcycle technician degree. The three boys and their mothers provided the contrast between the two distinct classes of Milan—the haves and the have-very-littles. Vicki Altieri wore a bright pink sweater with jeans, and her hair was wild with overdying and the effects of cigarette smoke. Jamie stood next to Ethan and Alex—two kids headed to college next year, two kids involved in sports every season and in the National Honor Society—and smiled. He had something to be proud of too.

After the senior night ceremony came to a close, Josh retreated to the locker room with the boys. He wanted to position that night's game as meaningful preparation for Hauser in the tournament, nothing more. This wasn't a conference game, and because Union County would play their tournament games further north and Milan would head south, it was unlikely that the two teams would meet in the tournament. Milan had prepared for Union County simply because they did things very close to the way Hauser did things.

Josh took a marker and wrote on the board: PRIDE PASSION POISE EMOTION. They were four words that anyone might struggle to connect to the 2010–11 Milan Indians. Pride? In what? Passion? Apart from a few flagrant fouls out of frustration, the team showed little. Poise? Milan was averaging 22.9 points in the first half of games while their opponents averaged just 2.2 more. But when the second half came, when foul trouble and talent and aggression and coaching took over, they were outscored by nearly five points. Emotion? The emotion seemed to come after games, and only for Ethan or Braden, and sometimes Kurtis.

"The bottom line, gentlemen," Josh said after he wrote the words on the board, "is what you do in the tournament. Tonight is a good test because Union County's a lot like Hauser. Those third quarters we've been having? Can't be that way. We have to go out and play Milan basketball!"

As the boys gathered into the huddle, they wondered what exactly Milan basketball was. For the past year, they had been told about the Milan way, but how did that translate on the floor? Ethan, Alex, and Braden had something to think of as Milan basketball—their family covered most of Milan basketball history. They were the ones mimicking the Pierceville Alleycats, shooting baskets in the cold at their grandfather's until they were nearly frostbitten or until it was time to head to the high school with their parents to watch the mighty Milan Indians. But what did Milan basketball mean to the rest of the team? What did it mean to Kurtis, who had struggled all season to live up to the promise he showed as a sophomore? What did it mean to Nick Ryan and John Herzog, dependable but quiet kids who never seemed to be affected by the outcome one way or another? What did it mean to Zack Lewis, the quarterback of the football team and catcher for the baseball team, to come out in a tank top during the winters and lose and lose, unlike in fall or spring?

There was a time when Milan basketball meant something, could be defined. That was before Ethan or Alex or Zack or John or Nick or Braden or Kurtis was born. For most kids—unless they were a Voss or unless they were indoctrinated early—Milan basketball was just a way to pass the time between football season and baseball season, a speed bump in the school's athletic success. The banners still hang on the wall, but few remembered who put them there.

After Stephanie Kirk put the finishing touches on "The Star-Spangled Banner," the referee walked up to her and said, "You sounded just like Dolly Parton. You just made my night."

It wasn't just the national anthem that seemed better that night. Despite John Herzog getting himself into foul trouble, Milan stayed with Union County in the first half. Josh let John play because, as he yelled to John, "If we're in the sectional championship and you have two fouls, I can't take you out!"

The Milan players seemed to have surprised themselves in the first half. Josh waved for Kurtis to come talk to him as Braden shot a free throw, and Josh told him that he read the play well on the previous possession. Kurtis, thinking he was about to get yelled at, didn't quite know how to take the compliment.

As Milan took their first lead of the game with six minutes left in the second quarter, it had become clear that Union County hadn't prepared for them at all. Milan went into halftime up 21–18, and Josh met the team at half-court, clapping his hands emphatically. Josh and Milan needed this game, needed some sort of momentum to carry them into the tournament.

In the locker room, Josh was sure to warn the boys about what they faced in the second half. "They've settled," Josh said. "He's over there telling them to stop shooting threes and go inside." Josh wanted to stay with the zone because it was their only hope of staying with the bigger, more athletic Union County players, but they needed to start rebounding. "I'll give you all the help I can," Josh said, sitting down next to Ethan and Alex on the bench. He rarely sat during halftime, and seemed to be leveling with the players. "I think they're pushing you in the back a little. I'll point it out when I can." The boys perked up at this. "Yeah!" most of them said under their breaths. It was the most relaxed halftime of the year.

Josh sent the boys out on the floor with this message: "You're in the best spot you can be in. Now you just have to take care of the ball." The boys, in some ways, were in the best spot they could have been in for living in a place like Milan. Ethan was headed to Purdue next year and hoped to manage the basketball team. Alex was off to DePauw University to play football and study journalism. Despite their depressed corner of Indiana, they had achieved something, basketball be damned.

17

HOPE

End of Regular Season: 5–15

After Milan shook hands with Union County following the 50–42 loss, Josh Blankinship did something he hadn't done in the previous nineteen regular-season games. He kept walking. Usually after shaking hands with the opposite team, he would turn back to the larger stairwell leading out of the Milan High School gym, away from the state championship banner on the west end of the gym, and toward John Prifogle's perch against the movable wall on the east end of the gym. But after looking up at the three members of Union County's frontcourt who outrebounded the Indians 11–4 on offensive rebounds, Josh seemed unable to face the normal eddy of screeching teenagers he would have to navigate through to get back to his office. And so he kept walking toward the exit on the opposite end of the gym. For a minute it looked like he might keep walking to his GMC Canyon pickup, get in, and never come back. He would open his truck door, turn on the GPS he kept docked on his windshield, and press "home." He'd pull out of the Milan High School parking lot, drive past the Jay-C Food Store and the Family Dollar, take a left at the flashing red stoplight, and point his truck toward Batesville. And where would that get him? He would arrive at the two-bedroom cottage on Lake Santee outside Greensburg that he rented from his boss.

He could have walked out on his job—those kids, those parents, that school— at that very moment, but even his home was so tied to his job that he could never really walk away from anything. And what would he do then, a twenty-eight-year-old physical education teacher and basketball coach, walking out on his first head coach job at a small school? Leaving would preclude him from moving up, and there wasn't much room to move down.

And so Josh Blankinship, the coach of the famous-for-the-past-but-not-the-present Milan Indians, turned back toward the court. He stood under the tattered 1953 state runner-up banner, the same water-damaged banner he rescued from the dank corner of a storage attic when he started his job sixteen months prior. Josh had been used to winning back then. He'd been an assistant coach at powerhouse New Albany and played at Anderson High School, whose gym, the Wigwam, sat nine thousand—the second-biggest high school gymnasium in the world. Josh looked back at the court where he had watched his famous team fail, just as they had all season, and just as they had since the fifties, it seemed. Maybe he thought better of leaving; maybe he was never going to leave at all; but at the last minute he ducked down the smaller staircase leading to the offices at the west end of the gymnasium.

Coach Theising and Coach Stutler entered the dark hallway and found a familiar shadow in the fluorescent emergency light: Josh, bent at the waist, butt leaning against the wall, resting his elbows on his thighs and interlocking his fingers.

"Our margin for error is zero," Tyler Theising started. To him, a first-year coach, the minutes after the last regular-season game were like any others. He, Stutler, and Josh would stall in the hallway, throw out the first things that came to mind about the game their boys just played, and cobble together a postgame script for Josh. But Tyler was absolutely right. This game only added to the staggering rebounding margin between Milan and their opponents this season. In their twenty games, Milan's opponents had 165 offensive rebounds— more than eight second chances a game. Milan had to play nearly perfect basketball to win.

"That team is *really* good though," Josh said, rubbing his eyes with the pads of his fingers. "I don't think we could have played it any differently."

The hallway conference was one of the shortest all year. For Josh, there was no sense in replaying the things that went poorly for Milan in that familiar second half when the game got away from them. After all, Union County wasn't in Milan's section, and this wasn't a conference game. In the scheme of things, the game didn't matter much. He charged into the hallway leading to the varsity locker room with a zeal he hadn't exhibited all season, not even after one of the five wins.

"Being 100 percent honest, you need to put your heads up," Josh said as he pushed open the locker room door. He had no way of knowing how much his words would sound like a command rather than an affirmation. After the words had left his mouth, he looked around and surveyed the locker room. Alex Layden had a towel over his head and was slumped over. Ethan Voss leaned back, staring up at the water-stained ceiling of the musty locker room. Next to him, his brother Braden had his face in his hands, his body heaving as he struggled to breathe through his sobs. It was his brother's and cousin's senior night, and he had made a couple of errors down the stretch in the fourth quarter that could have—in his mind—set the game right for Milan.

Ethan and Alex were upset, but the kind of upset that was self-pitying—not aimed at Braden or even the game itself. It was senior night, and Alex and Ethan simply had wanted to win their last game on their home court. It wasn't about the specific game for them—it was about the ability to say, fifteen or twenty-five years down the road, that they left as winners. It was the type of thing Braden couldn't understand because he didn't have to face leaving Milan for another year. His tears showed that he thought he could have won the game for the team, for his family's seniors, for the school, for the whole damn town. It was about the specific game for Braden, not the blurry, pithy memories to be told years later. He gasped as if all 1,816 Milan residents were sitting on his chest.

"Listen, get your heads up," Josh said. It was a line he delivered often postgame, and usually it was accompanied by a tone of anger, as if to say *Be a man. Face what happened.* But now, as the clock pushed 10 p.m. due to the senior night festivities before the game, his words were those of a soothing mother.

"Did we have a few errors?" Josh asked. "Yeah. Heck, yeah, we did. But we didn't lose, they won. There's nothing you can do about that."

Josh felt like he had to point out a couple of instances down the stretch that affected the final outcome of the game. As he did, Coach Theising had a moment of inspiration. He walked over to the whiteboard, unknown to the players and Josh, and erased the halftime instructions. Tyler was just two years removed from his senior year at East Central High School and knew perhaps better than anyone on the coaching staff what a player needed to think about in late February in Indiana.

On the board, Tyler wrote in large letters: *YOUR RECORD is now 0–0!!! NEW season starts NOW!!!*

Under the message, filled with all sorts of hope for the tournament, Tyler time-stamped it, as if the message would never be erased, as if he had carved it into the wall forever: *9:45 PM 2/25/2011*.

"Listen, guys, our margin for error is so small. You saw that tonight. But you couldn't have played it any differently. Understand this, though." Josh was done with the regular season, in just two minutes of postgame talk. It was time for Hauser and the tournament, even tonight in the wake of another loss. "That team is two times better than Hauser ever thought about being. It would not surprise me one bit if Union County won their sectional."

The Milan players looked up at Josh in unison. Suddenly, they lost interest in those marks on the floor they'd been looking at, those scuffs on their basketball shoes they'd been focusing on so intently. All ten players looked up and met Josh's eyes as he said the one thing they needed to hear.

"It wouldn't surprise me one bit if we win our sectional too."

They played well enough to win the game tonight, Josh told them. And it was true, for the most part. If Milan was ever going to beat a team whose starting lineup outsized them by a full foot—like Union County's did—the effort they gave that night was what it was going to take.

What Milan was willing to look past—maybe for the purposes of positive thought, or maybe they weren't even willing to consider it at all—was that Union County came into the game unprepared. Milan, for the most part, had done a good job of stopping Union County's regular offensive sets, and the result was an eight-point Milan loss. What would have happened if Union County *had* prepared? It wasn't a question anyone in that locker room was going to consider.

Josh turned to the whiteboard as he finished his pep talk and started to write the practice time for the next day when he saw Tyler's note.

"What Coach Theising has written on the board is the thing that should make you excited about being a high school basketball player in Indiana," Josh said. "You played good enough to win tonight. We didn't. But none of that matters now. You're 0–0. Everyone in the state is—Park Tudor is, Union County is, Hauser is. Tomorrow, at 11 o'clock, we start on Hauser." Josh collected the boys in their usual postgame huddle. "State on three. One, two, three."

"State!" the boys yelled. As the coaches turned to walk out of the locker room and into the coach's office, Braden still couldn't stop crying. He dug his face into his cousin's bare shoulder and wept.

When Josh went out to the court where families and friends were gathered to talk after the game, he walked over to Brian Voss, who was talking to John

Herzog's dad. These were the last two men anyone would have expected Josh to seek out after a loss. Yet Josh walked right up to them on the bleachers next to the scorers' table Brian had operated that night.

"Listen, Brian, you need to pat Braden on the ass when you get home," Josh said.

"Pat? Or kick?" Brian said with a smile. He'd been a star player for Milan in the late seventies and early eighties, keeping in the Voss family tradition. Brian's dad had played for Milan, his older brother David was "Mr. Ripley County" for the Indians, and his younger brother Brad had played for Milan too. He knew Braden made some mistakes down the stretch but had no idea how Braden had taken things in the locker room after the game.

"No," Josh said. "Pat."

Brian wasn't used to Josh ending conversations like this. Usually the roles were reversed—Brian would offer some sort of suggestion about the way the boys should play, and the conversation would end there, with Josh not knowing how to respond to such prescriptive advice and Brian thinking he got through to Josh because of the silence. Josh walked off right after he told Brian to "pat," and Brian nodded as if to say: *Yes, sir, I will do that,* his nonverbal agreement aimed right at the back of Josh's buzz-cut head.

On March 2, if you walked the halls of Milan Senior High School, you wouldn't have known that the first round of the sectional for the most storied high school basketball team in the most storied basketball state in the country was happening that night. Apart from the paw prints on the varsity players' lockers, there were no streamers or balloons or much to indicate that the Milan Indians were going into the tournament they made famous in the 1950s.

In H. G. Bissinger's account of the 1988 Permian High School football season, *Friday Night Lights,* he includes pictures of the high school and the town. During the regular season even, Odessa, Texas, overflowed with Panther Pride—their rallying cry "MOJO" was written on store windows in shoe polish, and signs displayed in the yards of every player let the town know that a Panther lived within. In the 2004 documentary *Friday Nights in America,* it looks as if students could barely walk through the halls of Permian High during the fall—MOJO signs and white and black balloons filled the hallways. But the Permian Panthers win—they have six state championships and two national championships to their credit. It was hard to show such enthusiasm when Milan entered the tournament 5–15, even if it was an improvement from their 3–17 record the year before. In the 2008–9 season, Milan was 4–17. In 2007–8, they managed only one win, and they hadn't had a winning season since 2003–4. History only takes a team—and a fan base, it seems—so far.

Even the cheerleaders had seemed to forget about the tournament. Early on the day of the game, Josh walked through the halls and asked Stephanie Kirk about the plan for the pep session later that afternoon. There was no plan.

Still, the students packed the gym twenty-five minutes before the end of the day. The cheerleaders stood on the court in front of Milan's four hundred students, all seated in the north bleachers. Even though the entire school and teachers were required to attend the pep session, the crowd seemed small in the two-thousand-plus-capacity gym. Most students sat in groups of their friends, ignoring the cheerleaders in their black-and-gold football uniforms with "CHEER" across their chest and the last two digits of their graduation years as jersey numbers. Football jerseys during basketball season—a perhaps unintentional message sent by the cheerleaders in support of the school's successful football program. Unlike the football team, which had played in the region final just months ago, the basketball team hadn't made regionals in eight years.

Josh walked out onto the gym floor wearing one of the gold shooting shirts the basketball team wore during warm-up, tucked into black jogging pants. The quickly thrown together plan created by the cheer team involved some of the school's faculty scrimmaging the basketball players in the last half of the pep session to give the school some hope for the varsity team later that night.

Stephanie Kirk addressed the crowd over the PA system. "Okay, everyone, Mr. Blankinship is going to come out here and talk about team and talk about what the game strategy is, so everyone give it up for Mr. Blankinship!"

Josh sauntered over to the microphone. "I need all varsity basketball players to come out here at half-court." The ten varsity players walked to midcourt, leaving Patrick Baker and Ben Lawhorn—the two JV players who were dressing for sectionals—near the usual bench area of the gym. "And the two who are dressing tonight. Baker, Lawhorn, get out here." Josh had fretted over which two JV players would fill out the twelve-man tournament roster. Other than Logan Alloway and Jake White, who had been playing both varsity and JV that year, none of the players were really good enough. Patrick Baker was the most consistent post player for the JV team. The varsity could use him in practice: he was a big kid known for playing a bit rough, and he could help the varsity prepare for the bigger teams like Hauser in the sectionals. Ben Lawhorn was a ceremonial choice—he was the only junior not playing varsity minutes. Coach Theising and Coach Stutler were surprised earlier that week when Josh said he was going to select Lawhorn for the tournament roster. Lawhorn, toward the end of the JV season, wasn't even starting. Dressing for sectionals would be Ben's swan song, a thank-you for his hard work as a kid in the Milan basketball program.

Josh introduced the seniors to the crowd, then the rest of the team to sparse applause. The biggest applause came for Logan Alloway, the sole freshman on the team.

"Now, I can sit up here and talk about game plan, but that stuff's really not important," Josh said, looking through the crowd. "The bottom line is: How many of you all are going to show up tonight? That is the key." He thanked the crowd for their attendance at their last win, the Scottsburg game.

"That game had nothing to do with what these guys did. That just goes to show that the more of you show up to support the team, the better they'll play."

The kids looked stunned. One student yelled, a little louder than what was polite, that he wouldn't be there. It wasn't the reaction Josh was hoping for, and he wore the disappointment on his face. He looked old all of a sudden, far beyond his twenty-eight years. He looked every bit as tired as he had after the Scottsburg game, when he looked like he was about to throw up from exhaustion in the locker room. He changed tack.

"That said, these guys have a lot of expectations. Expectations put on them, but also expectations they put on themselves."

Again: silence. Any expectation put on the team wasn't coming from their peers. The players had heard it all day in class, their peers bluntly telling them that they were probably going to lose tonight. *Right? I mean, Hauser is pretty good—and they're so big! How bad did they beat you this season? Thirteen points?*

Out of ideas, Josh decided to go for the one thing he knew would get the crowd rowdy for the boys.

"I hope all of you can come out and support us tonight—teachers, students, administrators—and watch us get a win against the Hauser Jets. We'll be back here, same place, same time, Friday. But the only way we're going to be here is if we get a win tonight. The only way we get out of class twenty-five minutes early is if we get a win tonight. And if we get a win tonight, I'm going to see if Principal Healy will give us the whole eighth period off, so we'll see about that."

The Milan gym erupted as if a last-second winning shot of the state tournament had just been hit in front of the students. Josh handed the microphone back to Stephanie Kirk.

"For those of you who are going to come out tonight—who *should* come out tonight—the game is at 6:30 at South Ripley High School. And the theme for tonight is 'Black Out,' so wear all black and . . ." Stephanie trailed off, "intimidate the crowd."

Stephanie went on to introduce the varsity team, which was going to take on the faculty team. The lights were off, and the spotlight searched the floor, just as during the home varsity games, but the gesture seemed a bit silly without the pep band playing and the organic buzz of a real game. After they were introduced, Zack Lewis and Braden Voss ran over to the rim and took turns jumping and hanging on it, showing off for their peers. Stephanie introduced the faculty team: Josh; the athletic director, John Prifogle; the girls' coach, Lisa Bradshaw; and the younger members of the Milan faculty. Stephanie returned the microphone to the scorers' table, where she put it up to a stereo playing rap music.

The pep session game was a bevy of backboard passing and strutting from the varsity team. The faculty team were hopeless against the varsity players, mostly because the faculty had trouble getting up and down the court. Even Josh, a pretty good athlete in his day, started to breathe hard about one minute in despite the game's slow pace. Midway through the game, frustrated at the varsity team's early lead, Josh dribbled to the volleyball line, pushed John Herzog out of his path, and shot a long three-pointer. It hit the backboard.

With the varsity up 14–0, the faculty had all but given up. They were sweating, resting with their hands on their knees, letting the varsity players show off with behind-the-back passing and circus layups.

And then it happened.

Lisa Bradshaw shot a jumper and missed. Prifogle collected the rebound and put up another shot, missing. A teacher who looked athletically unable to tie his shoes, let alone play basketball, collected the rebound and threw up another shot, missing. Blankinship rebounded. Another putback missed. Bradshaw rebounded. If the varsity team let the faculty have a string of four offensive rebounds—admittedly, in a pep session game—how would they fare against the big, athletic Hauser Jets?

At the end of the eight-minute mock game, the students filed out of the gym to their cars and buses, ignoring the varsity basketball players on the court, ignoring Kurtis Kimla—the one player on the team who could dunk—swooping in from the left wing to attempt one-handed jams, ignoring the boys with those historic words "Milan Basketball" across the chests of their T-shirts.

After the pep session, Josh went back to the office to shave in his private bathroom and change for the game. He sat in his office chair in his jogging pants, shirtless, his initials tattooed on his left shoulder in old English script. He had a habit of checking that night's matchups around the state before his game, keeping an eye on New Albany and his alma mater, Anderson. Anderson had probably just played the last regular-season game in their famous gym, the Wigwam, though that wouldn't be final until early March, when the Anderson school board decided they didn't have the funds to operate the nine-thousand-seat stadium anymore.

Before Coach Stutler could even sit down at his desk, Josh was complaining. Stutler taught seventh- and eighth-grade history, so he didn't know about the high school pep session. "They had nothing planned until midday, Jeff," Josh said. He walked into the bathroom to start shaving. As he dipped his razor under the faucet, his face was red even before he started irritating his skin.

"I guarantee if we were 15–5 instead of 5–15, there'd be all sorts of stuff up like the football team had."

Jeff took off his black Milan football jacket and slung it over the back of his office chair.

"You going to the Methodist Church to eat?" Jeff looked embarrassed by the football team's success in light of the rough basketball season, since he was the offensive coordinator. Changing the subject to the Methodist Church pre-game meal seemed like a pretty good option.

"I haven't gone all year, Jeff," Josh said, rubbing aftershave gel into his neck. "Why start now?"

"Maybe that's why we're 5–15, then," Jeff said, smiling.

Three of the players' mothers had decorated the locker room and coaches' office the night before. They put cartoonish signs on the locker room door that depicted a tiger dribbling a basketball with "Cruise to the hoop for 2!" in the top left corner. Each player, coach, and manager received a goodie bag, a brown paper bag with stencil cutouts of basketballs and words like "Win!" or "Play Hard!" pasted onto the outside. Inside, they put a bag of pretzels, a Kool-Aid pouch, and other treats.

The mothers also loved teasing Josh, who was in most cases fifteen years younger than they were. When Josh came into work that morning, three Barbies with homemade Milan cheer outfits—black skirts and yellow sweaters with black-markered Ms—sat on his office chair. Their legs were spread, their underwear and shoes on Josh's keyboard. One Ken doll sat on his chair as well, presumably representing Josh. A homemade card on his desk read "Here's hoping a win falls in your lap."

18

BOTH LION AND LAMB

The State Tournament: 0–0

Josh stepped into the bus wearing the same black-and-yellow sock cap he had worn to each away game that season. If someone didn't know about his ear problems, how the wind whipped through his ear canal and caused his ear to throb, caused it to drain all that blood, and how it was at its worst in the hours leading up to a game with all that stress—especially in the first round of the most hallowed high school basketball tournament in the world—the cap would look a bit out of place. The weather in southeastern Indiana had turned, as it does sometimes out of nowhere, unseasonably mild. The snow and ice that had kept the Milan students out of school for five days already that year had melted that afternoon, thanks to the 52 degree weather that had the boys sporting T-shirts on the bus for the first time all year.

Tournament time in Indiana is a wild thing—it turns prepared coaches into tornadoes of scouting reports, new secondary options for old plays, and ideas for how to attack a two–three zone defense. Josh had climbed the three steps of the Milan School Corporation bus eleven times this season, each time hanging his dress clothes up on the window next to the second seat on the right side of the bus, then putting his gym bag next to it, and his briefcase in the first seat on the right-hand side, next to where he would sit. The second seat on the right side was not for players, not for coaches, not for jerseys, not for basketballs, not for managers, not for other coaches' gear. That second seat on the right side was for Josh's clothes and gym bag.

Josh sat in his seat, rifling through his briefcase.

"Okay, I've got Southwestern Hanover's folder and I've got South Ripley's folder." If Milan managed to beat Hauser that night, they would play the winner of Southwestern Hanover and South Ripley, who played the second game of the night. If Milan won, the coaches and some of the players would stay and scout that game, and Josh knew he'd need to be prepared.

Milan had shown that they could play with teams like Hauser, teams that relied on size. Milan seemed like a different team at this point—sure, their winning percentage was a little worse than the 2–3 record had showed heading into that game back in December, but after a win against Scottsburg, playing one of the best teams in Class 1A tough for a half, and taking one of the best teams in eastern Indiana down to the final seconds, the boys couldn't help feeling like they were playing their best basketball of the season. There's no better time than March for that to happen.

"You can look back and see who's nervous," Josh said, nodding at the boys, specifically Zack Lewis. Zack looked like the first boy ever comfortable in a school bus seat, head back, mouthing the words to a rap song on his headphones. "Zack Lewis? You kidding? No way. That's why he's a good quarterback." Tyler looked back at the boys, trying to figure out who Josh thought might be nervous. Two boys seemed to be the most likely—Braden Voss, leaning out into the aisle, head drooped and hands folded in between his legs, elbows resting on his thighs, and Kurtis Kimla, who was doing his best not to make eye contact with anyone or anything while at the same time trying not to focus in on any one thing in particular. Tonight would be Braden's first tournament game as a featured member of the Indians, but for Kurtis it would represent a new season after a disappointing decline in play during the regular season. Both needed to prove themselves for Milan to have success.

When the bus pulled up on Ice Rink Hill—the hill about three minutes south of Milan Senior High School, named for the ice rink the valley became in the winters—Josh's cell phone went off. There was little cell phone service at Milan High School. Phones received service in parts of the gym, and that was it. For instance, the managers set their cell phones on the left side of the scorers' table during practices. If the phones were positioned upside down, then they received one bar of service, enough to receive texts from those friends lucky enough to live in or drive through the small pockets of service in Milan. Jamie Altieri, the twenty-year-old senior manager, had a habit of propping his phone upside down on his bedroom windowsill. His phone received texts from that position, then he would reply from his bed and prop the phone up in the same position during the sending process. But other parts of Milan—the rest of the school building, most of the homes—were void of cell phone contact.

Brian Voss had sent Josh a text that morning from his Batesville State Farm Insurance office. Josh had flipped open his phone to read "Good luck tonite! I honestly think we're as good as anyone there! When we want to be!"

Something in Brian and Josh's relationship had turned. While Brian had been happy for his son Braden earning a starting position on the team, he was upset that it had come at the expense of Ethan's starting role. Throughout the season, Brian had—through e-mails, texts, phone calls, and in person—expressed concern that Josh was "mistreating" Ethan in his senior season. What made those conversations with Brian so tough for Josh was that Ethan was a quiet leader, but a leader nonetheless. There wasn't a moment in practice or in a game where his effort was suspect or his body language demonstrated a kid who had given up on the team's season or his own high school basketball career.

It's probably why Brian had been so upset with Josh earlier in the season. Ethan had played big minutes the year before and was seen by the team, the school, and the community as a leader. Why sit a kid like that on the bench? Earlier, Brian had been a part of the group of parents who would get frustrated with Josh during and after the games. But as the year went on and Braden emerged as an important member of the team, Brian's stance on Josh softened, at least publicly. Brian, when he wasn't keeping the book at the scorers' table, would choose a seat on the other end of the gym from that group of parents—the Herzogs, Joey Davis's dad, the Walters—and keep mostly quiet during the game. It seemed his frustration earlier in the season was reduced to heartbreak for Ethan in his last season of high school basketball. All of a sudden, Brian's anger produced less criticism and more tender feelings for both of his sons.

While the team dressed, Josh took a lap around the court. He was careful not to step on the court—in tournament play, teams have only a certain amount of time to be on the court, and he didn't want to test to see if that rule extended to coaches as well. It was twenty minutes before Milan was allowed to take the court. He sauntered, shuffling side to side as he took a walk around the lines, with his head down, nervous. About twenty or so early fans were already in the gym, some Hauser fans in all black, some Milan fans in mostly black and some yellow, but mostly green-clad South Ripley fans claiming their favorite seat for their 8 o'clock game against Southwestern Hanover. Josh and the rest of the Indians were no strangers to this building, a new, wide-set gym with the latest features: bright plastic bleachers that contoured to fans' butts, two large scoreboards, and plenty of green and white. South Ripley's gym was louder than most, partially thanks to the great turnout South Ripley always had in their student section and partially due to the echo the new gym created. But an hour before the tournament started, the only sound was that of the large ventilation fans in the top corners of the gym.

As players, coaches, and fans walked into the gym, most instantly looked up and around the edges of the building. It was clear to see why South Ripley had been chosen for the sectional site—the gym was larger than most in the area, newer, impressive. But in the first week of March in Indiana, everyone looked at his or her own gym as if it were St. Peter's or the Sistine Chapel. Fans scanned each girder; players inspected every banner; coaches were suddenly interested in fluorescent lighting. Anything to remember that quiet gym for a moment, the feeling of the beginning of something potentially great.

On that night, Milan could have started a run even more improbable than the 1954 state championship. Back in the fifties, Milan was a good team from a small town, but a team who had been there before as state runners-up in 1953. On that night in 2011? They were just a 5–15 team whose predecessors had had a movie made about them. Josh looked around the gym. If Milan could get hot, even if they could get out of the sectional, they would once again be the stuff of legend. In some respects, though, the same feeling was residing in the hearts of coaches in all sixty-four sectional sites around the state that Tuesday night. It was a symptom of Hoosier Hysteria: in order to keep one's mind off the game, coaches and players tried to soak in every little pregame detail.

As Josh walked past, one early South Ripley fan leaned over to another man in his sixties who had chosen a nearby seat in the second row. "Who you rootin' for?" the South Ripley fan asked his neighbor.

"Aw, just here to watch the games," he replied.

Josh shook his head and smiled. Indiana basketball was right where he'd left it as a player in 2000—the old men still came to watch the games, not caring who won or lost.

Josh wanted to get the guys relaxed before pregame. "Number one, there is zero pressure on you guys," he started, pacing the room, applying lip balm, then cleaning out his ears with a tissue—the things he did when he felt anxious. "There's none. There's really none. There's no pressure because everyone else in the state is getting ready to do the same thing you're about to do right now. The first game of the sectional, Tuesday night, 6 o'clock. So you're not the only ones. Hell, there's 150 teams out there getting ready to do what you're about to do. So it doesn't make any difference. You've played about forty games together—twenty in the regular season, twenty in the summer—so you've had a lot of time to grow and mature as players. Workouts in the spring, workouts in the summer, all of your practices from the start of November until yesterday. Had some good ones, had some bad ones, but your practices the past couple of weeks have been really good. And the good thing about that is that's when we need to be at our best. So all that stuff that took place before now put you in the position you're in tonight. Just like everyone else in the state. So, there's zero pressure."

Josh sat down next to Ethan Voss on the bleacher. "Just go out and play and have some fun," he said, leaning back, filling time until they could go warm up. "That's the bottom line. Because right now you can forget about all the other games, you can forget about your game against Lawrenceburg at the beginning of the year, you can forget about the Ripley County Tournament, you can forget about all of that stuff. Because that makes zero difference right now. You're zero and zero right now. And the good thing about starting all over again is when we started our season before, we started pretty damn good. And now you have a new season. It's a clean slate. Clean slate. And that's what makes it fun. Because that's what really matters. It's not about what you do in the regular season. It's what you do in the tournament. Because guess what? North Decatur was seventeen and three in the regular season. It doesn't make any bit of difference because they could come out Friday night and get beat and it's over. Their season is done. It's just a proven fact."

Some of the boys looked around at each other. Alex Layden caught Ethan Voss's eye as if to say it could all end tonight, but it could just as easily end next month in Indianapolis. In that moment, everything seemed possible to Alex and Ethan, as if God himself had already written an amazing script for one team and the boys were just there to find out who got to play the leading role.

"The defending state 2A champions gone. Done. Twenty-five and two last year, got beat last night, first game," Josh continued. "Done. Had a lot of guys back. Done. Hauser's really good. They're good, aren't they? Sims is good, right? Miller's good. Guess what—we got good players, too. A lot of good players. So it's not about what's happened before, it's about what's about to happen in about two minutes."

A tournament official leaned into the door of the locker room. "Got the floor, coach!"

"That's what it's about, men," Josh said. "Clean slate, your new season starts tonight. Let's go."

After the boys had left the locker room for warm-up, Josh walked over to the full-length mirror near the door and put his suit coat on. Straightening his tie and his guardian angel pin, he looked himself in the eyes. "Fuck, we need a win tonight," he muttered.

If the boys had heard Josh's message, the simplicity of it was lost on them. The warm-up was a clinic on the many ways one could miss a shot. Air balls, short shots, all backboard, no rim, the Indians had them all. Their minds were playing clampdown defense on themselves. When the clock hit six minutes, the boys jogged back through the hallways of South Ripley High School to their locker room. For the first time all season, Josh had scripted his pregame speech.

"We're three games away from fulfilling a lot of dreams that a lot of people have," he said. It was hard to imagine him being wrong on that point—the Voss family alone would constitute a lot of people. Add to that everyone's parents, all the players, people like Linda White Baurley and Roselyn McKittrick back at the '54 Museum, and every Indiana resident just waiting to adopt Milan as their Cinderella team again—that was a hell of a lot of people.

"But now we just have to take advantage of that opportunity," Josh said, hands out from his body as if to say: *It's simple, we just have to do this easy thing.* "Three games away from fulfilling a dream—one of many—that a lot of people don't get to fulfill in the state of Indiana. We're going to be one of those teams that fulfills that dream, but we have to go one game at a time." The notion seemed to shock Braden Voss. When Josh mentioned that they would be one of those teams, Braden took a look around the locker room, ending at his older brother Ethan. He wanted nothing more than to be able to send his brother off to Purdue next year with a sectional championship.

"Take care of Hauser tonight, then we move on to Friday. Play hard, play smart, play together—and just remember, if nothing else, you're an Indian. I love you guys."

If March in Indiana enters—as the saying goes—like a lion and exits like a lamb, it was hard to tell which this night was, lion or lamb. After the pregame speech, the crowd that welcomed them as they took the floor for "The Star-Spangled Banner" was quite underwhelming. The South Ripley gym—capacity 2,400—was barely half-filled. Most of those in the crowd were South Ripley fans, waiting for the late game. Hauser fans had turned out in good numbers for a school about to be relegated to Class 1A from 2A because of shrinking enrollment. Despite having an hour longer to drive, Hauser had about four times as many fans as Milan at the beginning of the game. Most of their fans had called off the last few hours of work to travel to Versailles for the game, a luxury not afforded to Milan fans, who had only ten minutes to travel. The Milan fans would come, but a 6 p.m. start was simply too early for them.

After the national anthem, Josh had a few more words for the team before they were introduced. "Play every play like it's your last," he said, making sure his seniors Alex Layden and Ethan Voss were listening. "Because I'll tell you right now, there's no feeling like this in the world."

If Braden Voss could have articulated that feeling, sitting on the cushioned chair, waiting for the announcer to call his name for the starting lineup, it surely would have included the word "nervous." He looked up at his brother, standing with the rest of the nonstarters, and bounced his legs, shaking his upper body because he rested his elbows on his knees. Zack Lewis sat next to Braden and looked every bit the picture of relaxation, leaning back in his chair with his arms resting on the chair backs on either side of him. For Zack Lewis, it was just one more big moment. For Braden, it was a chance to show his brother how much he meant to him and how much basketball could still mean to the town of Milan, Indiana.

19

GRADUATION

Josh and Jill sat in the bleachers of the Milan High School gym, watching two boys cross the stage and accept their diplomas. Ethan walked up the steps toward his uncle, Marty Layden, and shook his hand a few minutes after Alex had accepted his diploma from Marty with a hug. The gym was decorated as well as one could decorate a cinder-block gym meant for basketball. In the corners of the gym, televisions on carts played a slideshow of senior pictures, baby pictures, and school events in the life of the class of 2011. The front of the gym was also the wall that held the 1954 state champs banner and the 1953 runners up banner. At the opposite end of the gym, the band was set up behind a removed partition wall. This was the wall that Alex had leaned against while catching his breath in practice. It was the wall that Ethan threw passes off in the corner, to simulate an inbounds pass. Catch and shoot. He must have done it a thousand times over the past four years. To the right of the 1954 banner, one of the moms had hung the class banner. *Nothing we do changes the past. Everything we do changes the future.* The motto was chosen by the class officers, led by Elaina Voss (president) and Ethan Voss (vice president).

The past. It was something Ethan wanted to reclaim his whole life, something he wanted to be a notable part of in the future. He sat in a folding chair that had been placed directly on the chipped wood gym floor—no tarp needed to protect the floor. On stage, the remaining members of the Milan High School Class of 1942 were crossing the stage to receive their diplomas. Four members were pushed in wheelchairs, including the only surviving male, Leroy Edens. The fifth and final member of the class, Gloria Hensley, walked. An outbreak of scarlet fever had prevented them from celebrating their commencement sixty-nine years before.

What mattered to Ethan was the history nearly three months in the past. The tournament game had been characteristic of their season in every way: up at the end of the first quarter, tied at halftime, and beaten by the end of the third quarter. Milan had played Hauser the way they had to play them, but Milan—Braden especially—missed shots they usually made. Poor shooting led to mental errors, and Hauser collected all the rebounds they could handle in the second half. As Alex and Ethan sat on the bench with towels over their heads in the final seconds, crying, the gym was taken over by the green and white of South Ripley and the red, white, and blue of Southwestern Hanover. "The hardest part is to know it's over," Ethan said to Alex. The tournament charged on. No one stopped the proceedings to wonder why Milan, once again, would not be moving on in the tournament they made famous.

The scene in the hallway at South Ripley High School was hectic that night. As the Milan team retreated into their locker room near the auxiliary gym, they seemed unsure of how to proceed. Josh told Tyler and Jeff that he needed to take a minute and tried to wade through the celebrating Hauser fans and through the South Ripley and Southwestern fans, full of hope for the result of the late game. As a group of excited and loud South Ripley cheerleaders passed him, he stood on his toes to look for his wife. The hallway was too crowded, and after five minutes of trying, Josh knew he had to go back and talk to those boys.

Ethan and Alex had their chance to say good-bye to the team in the South Ripley locker room, which still smelled of fresh paint. Until he heard his brother speak, Braden had held it together. But as he listened to his brother talk about how special Milan basketball would always be to him—had always been to him—Braden broke down. After Braden had played his way into his older brother's starting position, he promised himself that he would use his extra playing time to realize his brother's dream. Instead, he managed only one for six from three-point range in the biggest game of his brother's life. Ethan had similar trouble, missing all three of his attempted three-pointers. *Nothing we do changes the past. Everything we do changes the future.*

Not long after, all the players in the Milan locker room were reaching for a towel for their eyes. Despite the odds, they had expected much. They had expected to earn their place in Milan history, and Josh's rhetoric had set them up for that expectation. *Return to Glory*, Josh had printed on the scouting reports all season. That year was supposed to start the return to glory. Back on the Milan floor in late October, that's what they had believed. They believed back then that they had the tools—the Voss boys would shoot straight, Herzog and Lewis would shut down the other team's best players, Nick Ryan and Kurtis would claw their way to ten points apiece when the other team started crowding Ethan and Braden. It was an easy dream to have in Milan, Indiana. It was easy to see the given collection of boys each year as a complete team, full of players who had roles to fill. The magic of the 1954 team, it seemed, was that there was no real magic: there was a game plan to stall and play tough defense and let Bobby Plump and Ray Craft make some shots.

After the seniors and the coaches had reflected on the season, it was time to snap back to reality. All at once, Josh had to turn off the emotion that he had fought off all season, that had come so easily watching Braden and Ethan embrace in the middle of the locker room. The junior varsity players had forms for Josh to sign so that they could ride home with their parents rather than take the longest and quietest ten-mile bus ride ever. Finally, as he collected the last of the forms, he saw Jill, waiting against the wall in the hallway. They hugged, and Jill kissed his cheek. Josh turned away from the crowd, thinner now that the South Ripley–Southwestern game had started. "I'm so tired of hearing 'your kids play hard,'" Josh told her. "I've heard that for two years." He wiped his last tear away as Alex came out of the locker room, unshowered and in his warm-ups. He hugged a couple of friends—friends who knew what a tough week this was for him, since he and his girlfriend had broken up earlier that week—and then toward his parents. Braden soon followed.

"We gotta start having some shitty kids," Josh whispered to Jill, leaning back against the wall and folding his arms. "I need to recruit some dumb ones. I can't do this every year."

That night, the boys cleaned out their lockers with no fanfare. Ethan and Alex, when they were done loading their practice clothes into their gym bags, headed into the coaches' office and sat on the couch as if they had done it before. As if they knew it was the thing to do after Milan loses in the tournament.

When Josh walked into the office, he looked younger, or perhaps Ethan and Alex looked older. "As long as I'm here I'll have to say this, I think," Josh told them. "It's hard to end a season when you love the kids you have." Josh instructed the boys to thank their parents. Josh told them that sports made them who they were—all sports, not just basketball. Life lessons, Josh said. They stayed in that office into the early morning hours, passing on the stories they were told, the stories that were told in that office since before any of the coaches or boys first set foot there.

As I listened to the stories, I couldn't help but try to decide for myself whether the history—the stories, the lore, the movie, the 1954 team—was holding them back or keeping them fighting. All season it seemed as if it was the former. Josh would stick with the 1954 style of basketball, and the boys wanted to play up-tempo. Then Josh would switch, and it was clear that the boys wanted to play up-tempo because they wanted to run from the history. The older part of the town was stuck in the past. The younger part, except for Ethan, was running so hard from the past that they didn't realize they were running to nowhere in particular.

"They always make you think they're going to win," my fiancée had said after watching one of the Milan games with me. "And then they find some way to screw it up."

As I listened to Josh tell the boys stories about playing in the Wigwam as a teen, I thought about what my fiancée had said. The past disillusioned more than just the people of Milan. It changed the expectations of everyone who knew about that 1954 team, whether through newspaper clippings or the story as it was adapted for *Hoosiers*. We love a David beats Goliath story because in our biggest dreams, the ones worth working for, we are always David. If we were Goliath, we wouldn't need to dream.

The thing we were willing to look past was that David had moved on to a different dream. In 1954 Milan, it was still possible for teens to move on to their own version of success. They weren't David in terms of their future, so they were free to be David on the court. Now? Alex and Ethan were the rare Milan boys who would be able to succeed. Once that meant staying in Milan or moving right back after college. Now that was unlikely. David didn't live there anymore.

As Josh and Jill sat under a tent in the Laydens' driveway, eating mashed potatoes and corn and graduation cake, the same stories were passed around again. They talked about how strict the director of the summer basketball camp was, and how Ethan and Alex were glad to not be going back. They talked about how they would miss basketball next year, when Ethan was at Purdue and Alex was at DePauw. They talked—as Jill leaned back in her chair and rubbed her just-emerging belly—about how in fifteen years a little Blankinship might get to experience it all. The hope of October. The cold of January. The renewal of hope every March. It was hard to tell where Milan would be when Noah Robert Blankinship tried out for the team in his freshman year of high school, in the year 2025. It was hard to tell where Noah would be, where Josh would be.

Return to glory, Josh had told the boys. If Josh had his way, Milan's place in the Indiana basketball hierarchy would be restored, and he would be leading the way. Because even with all the money problems at the school, and their recent tradition of losing, and the unrealistic expectations of the parents, basketball in Milan still meant something. It meant something to the boys, and it meant something to the town. Over time, what basketball meant shifted—from anecdote to focal point to albatross and back to anecdote again—but it was never gone from the conversation about Milan. For Hoosiers, Milan still meant *Hoosiers.* Milan still meant miracle. The town still meant that, every now and then, hard work outlasted talent. The principal's message to the graduating class of 2011 underscored that idea: "Bill Gates and Steve Jobs didn't finish college." Even if the 1954 level of success was no longer feasible in Milan, it produced hope in other corners of the state, other corners of the Midwest, other corners of the country. Even if Plump's last shot had become a cliché in Milan, it still held meaning elsewhere. Josh was determined to restore that shot's meaning, even if it made him the smallest of Davids.

EPILOGUE

The Fall of David, the Resurrection of Goliath
December 2012

T̲his time last year, Josh's ears would have been aching. The parents
would have been after him, the team would have been losing without
much hope of fixing things, and Josh would have been wondering why he ever applied
to coach at the school whose history had diverged so far from its present reality
that it was hard for people to remember the difference between 1954 Milan and 1952
Hickory, between the real and the fictional, between the memory and the fable.

But something had changed with the Milan Indians over the summer.
With Ethan and Alex gone, the players in the rising senior class—one of the
largest in recent Milan basketball history—were free to set the tone for the team
themselves. They were free of Ethan's quiet, responsible, church-boy leadership
style. They were free of the tensions between Alex and some other members of
the team. They were free to play their own style: tough, rough, flashy. Milan was
actually winning, so much so that Braden bet his Uncle Brad that they would
finish the regular season with a 16–4 or better record.

Ethan Voss was home for Christmas break. The first semester at Purdue had
been difficult for him. As he sat in the stands watching his brother and his old

team beat Oldenburg Academy, he adjusted the flat bill of his 1980s retro snap-back Purdue hat. "It's not the workload so much," Ethan said. "I just didn't learn any study skills here." While Ethan and I watched the Braden-led edition of the Milan Indians, Jarrid McDonald stopped by to ask Ethan about school. Jarrid had recently graduated from Hanover College, just south of Milan, and Josh had created a volunteer-strength coach job for him. "Doing well," Ethan said. "Making a lot of ball games." He said he sat with the Paint Crew, the Purdue student section at men's basketball games, which was a play on head coach Matt Painter's name.

Earlier in the year, Ethan had missed out on his dream to manage the men's basketball team, which was a foolish dream in retrospect, since first-year students were rarely selected for the coveted positions. Hundreds of students applied each year. Ethan had hoped that his experience playing for the famous Milan Indians would give him an edge, that he'd be selected easily for the position with little resistance, similar to joining the Milan team. He didn't anticipate the experience to be like the tryouts for the Milan team in 1954, when fifty-eight of the school's seventy-three boys showed up to compete on the first day.

Ethan came home a few times that fall, once to see his cousin Alex when he was home from DePauw University and a couple of times to watch Braden play. Ethan hardly recognized this new Milan team. This team had swagger. Jarrid's weight-lifting program had produced a team that was a bit more physical. Several players could dunk, and they did so often in warm-up as a way of intimidating the other team. Toward the middle of the fourth quarter, Oldenburg had closed the Milan lead to single digits. Brian Voss leaned into the microphone at the scorers' table. "Let's hear you, Indian fans!" he yelled. Even the production of the game had shifted to more Indiana Pacer than Milan Miracle. Milan closed the game out with ease. As he watched his brother and his friends go through elaborate handshakes at center court, Ethan nudged my elbow. "I don't think they understand yet what it means to be from Milan. They will, but they don't now."

After the game, I went to Josh's office to catch up with him and Jeff and Tyler. I was excited because Josh had saved a ticket for Milan's next game for me—a rematch of the 1954 semi-state game between Milan and Crispus Attucks, to be played in the Hoosier Gym in Knightstown, the gym used as Hickory's home court in the movie *Hoosiers*. Members of the 1954 state championship team would be present, since the game was serving as a fund-raiser for the Milan '54 Museum, in hopes that it could move out of the old barbershop and into a more attractive, well-designed space in town. Roselyn McKittrick, the museum's curator, had her eye on the long-closed bank on the corner of Franklin and Carr.

Josh was excited too, and not just because, at twenty-nine years old, he was going to play out a childhood fantasy in a few days by coaching the Milan Indians in a famous gym. The previous day, Jill had given birth to Noah Robert Blankinship. Josh wanted to drive to Indianapolis the next day to scout Crispus Attucks with Tyler but wasn't sure if he would be able to. "Jill and Noah are coming home from the hospital tomorrow," Josh told Tyler and Jeff. "You know how she'll be. I'm not sure if I'll be able to leave."

Maybe his ears *were* starting to hurt. There was the baby and the game in the Hoosier Gym, but there was also a new expectation Josh gave himself: *you're winning now, so you better keep winning.* Josh noticed the reckless style with which this year's team was winning, the way they let their opponents know just how bad they were beating them. Off the court, there were issues: during the varsity game, a new junior varsity player was caught smoking marijuana in the parking lot. Josh decided that night that it would be that boy's last chance on the team. However, Milan looked a likely sectional champion for the first time in years, so none of these control problems were discussed between the administration and the parents. Winning was a soothing salve.

"Are we in the same locker room that Hugh Jackman was in?" Kurtis asked as the team stretched at midcourt while Josh, Jeff, and Tyler eased into jump shots on the rims they had seen so many times on their television sets.

Josh stopped his shooting motion. "Who did you say?"

"Hugh Jackman," Kurtis said. "When he gives that speech. Tells them he loves them."

The boys continued their stretching.

"Gene Hackman?" Josh asked, raising his right eyebrow. "And yes, that's the locker room. You'd know that if you had ever watched the movie."

Kurtis shrugged. He looked at Braden and said, "I tried. I fell asleep."

To the adults in town—and those outside the town who knew the story of the Milan Miracle—basketball was Milan's identity because it's what made the town special. To the kids, their relationships with each other were more important to their identity, because each other was all they had ever known. The camaraderie I witnessed among the students was unique and was directly tied to the remote location of Milan and the size of the student body. Linebackers played clarinet in the band. Basketball players were National Honor Society presidents. At school dances, students didn't retreat to corners of the room to gossip with friends. The senior class swayed to the music in a big circle, putting their arms around one another's shoulders. They didn't need history from sixty years ago. They were creating their own, together, and it was just as unique to Milan as a basketball win. When the Milan team first walked into the Hoosier Gym on game day, they were either listening to their music or goofing off. When Oldenburg Academy, which was playing Brebuf Jesuit Prep in the early game, came into the gym, they instantly knew to go to center court for a team picture with the famous scoreboard in the background.

The boys first realized that Josh's scouting report for Crispus Attucks was a lie halfway through the first quarter. As the boys leafed through the stapled pages, careful to not let the cheap copier paper stick to their fingerpads, they read that Crispus Attucks's point guard could make shots from the volleyball line and that he was the quickest player they would guard all year. Josh warned them of picked pockets and drawn charges.

The truth was that Josh couldn't afford the type of mental weakness that had plagued Milan in his previous two seasons with the team. The game at the Hoosier Gym was meant to showcase Milan, meant to raise money for the Milan '54 Museum. Knightstown was close to the middle of the state and close to Indianapolis, and the game was between Christmas and New Year's Day. People who were just curious about seeing Milan play in the gym they'd seen Hickory play in over and over in the movie could decide to stop in on a whim. Josh wanted to keep the secret from the state, let them keep on believing that in Milan, winter meant jump shots and motion offenses, meant Hoosier Hysteria, meant cheering on the best twelve boys in town every weekend.

I think Josh wanted to keep that secret from the rest of the state because it was something he'd believed in for so long. As he stood on the creaky stage looking out through the dust from the velvet curtain above the basketball court, Josh told a reporter that 1954 was the reason he took the Milan job. "People care about this team, this town. What those men did sixty years ago is the reason why I'm here, the reason why people in this state care so much about basketball." What if everyone knew the secret that everyone in Milan seemed to know but was so loath to acknowledge—that 1954 was a fluke and would never be repeated? That a movie was made to inspire hope in basketball fans, coaches, and players in every corner of the state, but the movie's message was hollow in the cold, harsh light of reality? Josh came to Milan as an outsider, as a believer in the sermon on faith he heard every time he cued up *Hoosiers* or read a news article that included the 1954 championship as an aside, as a brief reminder of what average boys from below-average towns could accomplish. How could he tell all those people—how could he let a poor game from his team deliver the message—that the god of winning small-town, stall-it-out, disciplined cut-and-screen basketball was never really alive at all, or at least was at one point but not any longer?

It was a god he wanted his son—his small, still wrinkled, eight-day-old son Noah—to be able to call on in fourteen years as he started his high school basketball career. He wanted Noah to age several years and stay that age for a long time, stay young enough to be coached about basketball, stay watching *Hoosiers* for the first time. He wanted his son to believe that he could reach into his sack, finger a stone, sling it, and kill the Philistine.

Milan won the game in the Hoosier Gym easily, by twenty points. It was not an upset: Crispus Attucks, deep in the impoverished northwest side of Indianapolis, was undercoached, underfunded, and undersupported. Milan would continue their regular-season success, finishing with a 15–5 record. In the big moments, though, Milan fell short. They lost in the county tournament and exited the sectional tournament in the second round.

The week after the game in the Hoosier Gym, before returning to Purdue, Ethan Voss drove past Milan Elementary School. The Voss family had paid for a concrete slab and two basketball goals at the edge of the schoolyard, in Papaw Hank's memory. Kids in Milan should have open access to basketball, the Vosses thought.

"It's the first time I had ever seen anyone playing on the court," Ethan told me. "I slowed down and watched this kid shoot." For a moment, Ethan didn't wonder why the boy was all alone, why he didn't have friends or brothers or cousins to join him. For a moment, all Ethan thought about was how it had all been worth it: learning to use your legs, keep your elbow in, keep your eye on the rim, and just let a shot fly. It was worth it to think it should go in every time, despite the previous misses. Once, a shot went in. It might happen again if someone keeps shooting.

POSTSCRIPT

F our years later, the poster above Josh Blankinship's desk still looms over the office. Out there, down the cinder-block hallway, under the stands and to the side of the court, with the buzzing fluorescent lights calling attention to the big case-enclosed class banner with the scars that not even the Indiana Historical Society could heal—even though they tried—it's tough to remember that this game, in this town, is heaven for some. But in Josh's office, even with the messy piles of plays and scouting reports and basketball summer camp fliers, the poster with that picture of that gym reminds you of what the game can be.

It's easy, at times, to remember that it's just a game. The end of another five-win season in a town known for a big win a long time ago, for instance, is a good time to remember that basketball can be a job, a passion, a life, but it's also just a game.

But it's also easy, when you see the poster above Josh's desk calling for a "Return to Heaven," to forget that it's just a game. When you see the Hoosier Gym on that poster, an old gym hours away from Milan that is most famous for being a movie set, it's hard not to conflate putting a ball in a basket with a town's identity.

When people find out that I've written a book, I have a simple way to tell them what it's about.

Me: "Have you seen the movie *Hoosiers*?"

They usually say yes.

And then I explain that *Hoosiers* is based on a real story that happened to a real team in a real town, and that real town still has a real team, but things are different there now. I explain about rural economics and the cultural meaning of basketball in Indiana, and about how every March news cameras and reporters go down to Milan to ask some really nice people about a team that once played there, a team that made history. Finally, I get to those really nice people, and how they're just trying to do their best at the thing that once made their town the best.

Sometimes I feel like I'm a part of the problem. How easy would it be to start with those really nice people for once? How there are some people who live in a small town near the Ohio River who care deeply about their kids making something of their lives, and who want those kids to be known for something. And, yes, things are really tough for a lot of them because a bunch of families used to farm, but you can't really make a living doing that by yourself anymore, and in a small town if one family suffers, then everyone suffers, but still they mostly make it even if it's not "making it" by somebody else's standards.

It's Milan's curse and it's Milan's blessing to be known for a team that played a season that inspired a movie that most everyone has seen.

For instance, Milan's legend keeps its sons close to home. I remember talking to Jarrid McDonald back in 2011. We were in the bleachers, watching Logan Alloway goof off. As Logan flipped the ball to himself on a wing, heaving a fade-away three-pointer, Jarrid shook his head. Jarrid had been both around Milan—he was a former player, back in Milan to help in the weight room while he was in college down the road at Hanover—and outside of Milan enough to know that Logan was something special. But instead of the disciplined practice character-istic of a small-town Indiana phenom, Logan was taking shots he'd never take in the game. Sure, he was making most of them—that was Logan's native talent taking over. He was simply goofing off rather than trying to elevate his game.

"You don't realize how special of a place this is until you leave," Jarrid said. "We grow up hearing about Bobby Plump and *Hoosiers*. You can tell it means something to people around here, but until you leave you don't realize what it means to people out there."

Four years later, Logan Alloway is the next generation of young adult to realize just what he had. He's gained about twenty pounds of muscle since he was fif-teen, but he's hung on to his soft-spoken confidence. As the freshman coach at Milan, Logan has come full circle from his recent past.

His junior year started with a suspension, and Josh didn't know if Logan had it in him to commit to the rules—both the team's rules and the school's rules. Remember: this was the same Logan who missed his first high school game because he had skipped a class earlier in the day. Logan, even as a freshman, had transcendent talent for Milan. He was well on his way to wasting it when he started dating Maria Voss.

Maria was a cheerleader, and Ethan, Braden, and Alex Layden's cousin. Her dad played for Milan. Her sister played for Milan. Her cousins played for Milan, and for as long as she could remember, those boys were out back of Papaw Hank's house pretending they were taking the last shot to win the state finals. But Maria and the Voss family had rules. Not that Logan's family didn't—they were ever-present—but boys don't always listen to their parents. For Logan, they were rules worth following, and he stayed out of trouble enough to stay on the team, graduate, and attend a community college in nearby Lawrenceburg while he coached, in hopes of transferring to a four-year institution soon.

Still, Logan was really just a boy. On the practice planning sheet for the day before Milan's opening tournament game against North Decatur, Josh had written "Coach Alloway: GUIDE FROSH THROUGH PRACTICE . . . ALL OUR PLAYERS MUST CONTINUE TO LEARN HOW TO LOOK YOU RIGHT IN THE EYE WHEN YOU ARE ADDRESSING THEM AS A GROUP OR ON A ONE-TO-ONE BASIS. PLAYERS SHOULD HEAR AND ACTUALLY LISTEN TO WHAT YOU ARE SAYING WHEN YOU SPEAK." It wasn't that Logan didn't have good things to say. He had been Milan's best player for the past three years, and he knew what kind of trouble a teenager could get into. It was that once Logan crossed the stage in the Milan High School gym, he was an adult as far as the boys were concerned. And adults were to largely be ignored when you're on the freshman team, waiting for your chance to play for a five-win team.

Logan's old teammate, Logan Karstetter, was back in town. Known as the team's best defender and worst temper, Karstetter had joined the army after graduation. He had always strutted around the Milan gym, but now he had fresh ink on his rapidly growing arms. The army had been good to Logan's physique, so when Logan and Josh invited him to help prepare the varsity team for North Decatur's excellent post players, Karstetter jumped at the opportunity.

As Karstetter pulled his basketball shoes out of his army rucksack, he stopped a manager.

"Hey, get me a Mountain Dew," Karstetter ordered.

Logan Alloway, thankful for a reason to turn away from the early stages of the practice, jumped in.

"Yeah, get me one too," Logan said.

Logan Karstetter grinned.

"Don't get him one—he's the one with the coach's check. He's rollin' in it," Karstetter smiled, knowing that Logan made hardly any money for coaching the freshman team and that he'd be defensive about it.

"Shoot, he's the one with the fourteen grand or whatever," Logan Alloway said as the manager walked away, intending to get neither alumnus a Mountain Dew. Logan Karstetter preened. Enlisting in the army was the easiest way to make what passed for big money in Milan, and he was glad that everyone knew it.

After some warm-up drills, Josh took the team up to his middle school health classroom to watch film on North Decatur. Disembodied CPR dummy heads lined the windows.

"Now, I'm not going to sit here and show you five hundred clips," Josh started. "Because they all show the same thing." North Decatur's best player was Evan Wallpe, a bruising post player with a variety of patient but powerful moves. Milan did have a tall kid this year to guard him, Kyle Meyer, but he was more of a finesse player. Once again, Milan would play the underdog thanks to a lack of size.

"This is where the problem begins," Josh shouted to the quiet room. "Wallpe already has his position. It's over at this point." Josh shuttled through about thirty plays, all Wallpe layups. "He's big, and he knows how to score, guys."

The problems for Josh had not changed, but the way he dealt with them had. The Wallpes of the world were always already in position, and Milan was not. The season after I spent a year with Milan, they won sixteen games but lost in the second round of the tournament. Another losing record after that, then another sixteen-win season and early exit from the tournament in Logan's senior year. Milan had improved but still couldn't advance in the tournament they had made famous. Was Josh bothered by that? Absolutely. But he seemed to deal with it in a different way. Sure, he was still breaking things out of frustration—when I arrived at practice, the first thing Josh did was take me to his office and show me the chair he broke after Milan blew a big third-quarter lead to lose. But the ear problems, the stress? Gone.

My guess? Josh had some perspective now. His second son, Lucas, had just arrived. Coaches in the area knew what good work Josh was doing, even if it didn't mean results in March. Josh was feeling less like an outsider and more like a part of Milan. He and Jill bought a house. Four years ago, Josh was worried about keeping his job. Now, as I left the gym, Josh called to me, "Come back next year and write a sequel. We're going to be really good. We might win seventeen games." Josh and his family felt settled.

Part of that settling may have resulted in more realistic expectations for the Milan program. In 2010–11, Josh had instituted "Return to Glory" as the team's motto. Each practice plan and scouting report included the phrase at the top, in bold, gold capital letters. Josh had the dream—still does, somewhere inside of him—that Milan would recapture the glory days of Plump and the Pierceville Alleycats, of the cat-and-mouse offense winning the big one in Indianapolis.

Now, the team motto read "Grit 'n' Grind." Josh tweeted to his players using the hashtag #gritngrind. They broke down huddles with the phrase. Hard work, rather than a big dream, Josh thought. An attitude rather than an unfathomable goal.

Maybe that's where the hope lies for Milan: not in recapturing the past, but in preparing for the future. In the end, it's the discipline—the grit 'n' grind—that can get you one step better. As Logan Alloway knows, it's also the ability to lean on those you love to make something of yourself. Not focusing on a "return to glory" isn't about forgetting the past for Milan, it's about its young people looking within rather than behind them for a solution to the problems that face the town. Cat-and-mouse isn't possible in 2015. Things have changed since 1954, and the concept of what glory means to Milan, Indiana, has, too. Moving out from the shadow of 1954 into the light of the present day isn't sacrilegious. It might just be the thing that saves Milan after all.

BILL RILEY is a writer and teacher originally from Greenfield, Indiana. He graduated from DePauw University in 2005 and earned an MFA in creative writing from The Ohio State University in 2012. He currently works at Rose-Hulman Institute of Technology in Terre Haute, Indiana. His work has been featured in *Punchnel's, Prime Number,* and *Spry Literary Journal,* and he writes a beer column for *Terre Haute Living Magazine.* He lives in Terre Haute with his wife and son, and is working on his first novel.

★   ★   ★

Lightning Source UK Ltd.
Milton Keynes UK
UKHW03f0505300318
320269UK00002B/234/P